THOMAS EDWARD LAWRENCE

was .... of an
Irish .... gma of
bastardy lay heavily on this man who
was to become one of the
most outstanding figures in
recent history.

*What compulsion drove Lawrence, a
student of archaeology, to grasp his his-
toric role? Why did he ride across
Arabia's endless sands, huddle in nomad
tents, the self-appointed English emissary conferring secretly with the Arabs?
Why did he storm the citadels of the
English to plead the Arab cause to General Allenby? How did he endure capture and torture in Deraa? What untold
strength led him to escape and ultimate
victory?*

This biography tells his story—
the story of a man who achieved the
impossible, and who turned away from
the rewards of his labor when
recognition was at hand, retiring into
the obscurity from which he came
. . . a mysterious figure to the last.

Outstanding SIGNET Biographies

ACT ONE by Moss Hart
The famous playwright and director tells of his early life, from poverty-stricken boyhood to his first big Broadway success, in this fascinating bestseller.
(#T1849—75¢)

THE YEARS WITH ROSS by James Thurber
A superbly entertaining biography of Harold Ross, eccentric founder and editor of *The New Yorker,* by its most famous humorist. ". . . a superb memoir of a man, a magazine and an era in American journalism"—*Saturday Review Syndicate.* (#T2020—75¢)

THE SEVEN STOREY MOUNTAIN by Thomas Merton
The spiritual autobiography of a young man who withdrew from a full, worldly life to the seclusion of a Trappist monastery. (#T929—75¢)

THE NIGHT THEY BURNED THE MOUNTAIN
by Thomas A. Dooley, M.D.
Dr. Dooley's account of the founding of his jungle hospital, the growth of his organization MEDICO, and the beginning of his own gallant fight against cancer.
(#D1974—50¢)

CONTENTS

On 16th August 1888 at Tremadoc in Wales a second son was born to a Mr. and Mrs. Lawrence. Named Thomas Edward, he was in fact the illegitimate child of Sir Thomas Robert Chapman, 7th Baronet of Westmeath in Ireland, who had left his wife and four daughters to elope with the children's governess, a Miss Sara Maden. Chapman changed his name to Lawrence and moved from Ireland to Wales and from then on he and Sara Maden lived together as husband and wife.

Mr. and Mrs. Lawrence had five sons—Bob (M.R.), who became a medical missionary in China until 1935, after which he devoted his life to looking after his mother; Ned (T.E.), who became the legendary and controversial "Lawrence of Arabia"; Will (W.G.) and Frank (F.H.), who were killed in action in World War I; and Arnold (A.W.), who became a professor of archaeology at Cambridge and is today T.E.'s literary executor. Bob, the eldest, and Arnold, the youngest, are the only members of the family still alive. T.E. died of injuries from a motor-cycle accident in 1935, the father succumbed to the influenza epidemic in 1919 and the mother died in 1959 only two years short of a hundred years of age. T.E. was a year old when the family moved to Scotland and then later to the Isle of Man, Jersey and France. When he was eight they finally settled in Oxford where the boys were educated at the High School and later at the University.

A precocious youngster known for his omnivorous

reading, T.E. early acquired an interest in archaeology and in such related subjects as ancient architecture, heraldry, armour, old manuscripts, pottery and relics of all kinds. Gradually his interest concentrated on mediaeval castles and fortifications.

According to his own account, related in later years to intimate friends, he was about ten years old when his father told him the facts of his birth—that his parents were not and could not be married, because Lady Chapman would never consent to divorce her husband. This discovery seems to have instilled in T.E. an obsession to prove himself better than his fellows, to show that in spite of his background—which set him apart from all his friends and associates—he could excel them in every way. This compulsion was in part responsible for driving him throughout three quarters of his life to make superhuman demands upon his mind and body.

Yet the shadow of shame that, in this era of Victorian morals, lay across the Lawrence family's origins did not manifest itself in any way to the outside world, to which they gave the impression of being a most respectable as well as affectionate and closely-knit family. This was due in large part to Sara Lawrence, a Scotswoman with an outstanding character, a commanding personality and an iron will which T.E. inherited from her more than any other of her sons. A tremendous puritan, Sara was haunted throughout her life by the sin she had committed and sought to make amends by bringing up her children with love and affection but with the strictest discipline, reinforced by regular attendance at church and Sunday school.

The father, although a well-educated man, never took up a job, being born and raised among the squirearchy of Ireland to believe that his task in life should be to devote himself to good family management and a proper pursuit of sport in one form or another. He was a keen yachtsman, and a crack shot. In the latter part of his life he developed a craze for bicycling, which he indulged with his sons and especially with T.E., whose interest in mediaeval castles led them on several tours of England, Wales and, later, France in the summer holidays of 1906–08. In October 1907 T.E. went up to Jesus College, Oxford, and soon became celebrated there for such individualistic exploits as exploring subterranean rivers and climbing roofs at night. He also gained a reputation for involved practical jokes, for a vanity which compelled him to be "different" at all costs, and for an unquenchable thirst for knowledge in the out-of-the-way subjects which captured his interest—mediaeval chronicles, Russian novels, works about military tactics. In his preoccupation with archaeology, he had haunted the Ashmolean Museum since High School days, and had come to the attention of such celebrated archaeologists as Leonard Woolley and D. G. Hogarth, who was to become a second father to him as well as his principal guide and mentor in the archaeology and customs of the Middle East. Among the books for which Lawrence developed an infatuation was Charles Doughty's *Arabia Deserta,* a travel and exploration classic which was also to influence his future.

T.E.'s interest in old English and French fortresses next led him to Syria and Palestine in search of the castles of the Crusaders. In the summer of 1909 he set out through these countries on foot, lodging with the local inhabitants, driving his body to the limit, suffering from malaria and dysentery, yet developing an enchantment for the Middle East and its peoples that was soon to be the ruling passion of his life.

His immediate purpose was to write a thesis required by the University for a B.A. degree. This was later published under the title *Crusader Castles,* illustrated with his own photographs and sketches. He passed his final examinations brilliantly and, on the recommendation of Dr. Hogarth, was granted a research "demyship" by Magdalen College, which would pay living expenses and enable him to join, as an otherwise unpaid assistant, the British Museum's mission at Carchemish on the Euphrates, where an ancient Hittite city was being excavated.

To improve his knowledge of Arabic, he first attended the school of the American mission at Jebail, Lebanon, where Dr. Hogarth joined him and then took him on another reconnaissance of Syria. They reached Carchemish in March 1911 and here Lawrence worked for the next three years, collecting and classifying pottery, overseeing and directing the Arab and Kurdish workmen, living among them and learning their different dialects, their family histories and idiosyncrasies, and settling their disputes.

When summer heat closed down the "digs" in 1911, T.E. took off on another Syrian walking tour which ended in fever and exhaustion. But, after a brief recuperation at Oxford, he resumed work at Carchemish. There he remained for the next two years, with the exception of a brief interlude in the summer of 1913, when he returned to the family home at 2 Polstead Road, Oxford, with two Arab friends, Sheikh Hamoudi, foreman at Carchemish, and Dahoum, the water boy, with whom he had roamed the unknown corners of the desert. Scandalizing the Oxonians, he taught the two to ride bicycles in their Bedouin robes. A near-riot with an Egyptian student further outraged the citizens and the return of the trio to the desert was welcomed by all.

These experiences of Syria left a deep and lasting impression on the young Lawrence. He hated to see this gentle and beautiful land and its kindly hospitable people living under the heel of Turkish tyranny. The "Garden of the Enchantress," as he called it, should be cleansed of alien thorns and scorpions and allowed to blossom in freedom. Damascus, he vowed, must one day become the capital and centre of a free and joyful *Arabia Liberata*.

Meanwhile the Central European powers were spoiling for the fight that was to become World War I. Lord Kitchener, British Resident in Egypt, aware that Turkey would probably side with Germany in the event of war, was preoccupied with the defence of the Suez Canal, Britain's essential artery. The natural bastion for the defence of Egypt was the Sinai peninsula, under Turkish control and virtually unmapped. To disguise an attempt to reconnoitre the area, the Palestine Exploration Fund formed an expedition to look for the "itinerary followed by the Israelites in the course of the famous forty years which they spent in the desert." The expedition consisted of Woolley, T. E. Lawrence and a Captain S. F. Newcombe of the Engineers. The result of their work was a report, "The Wilderness of Zin," which they completed at Oxford and London in the summer of 1914. They were still drawing the maps to accompany it when war was declared.

Lawrence spent the rest of that year writing a guide of the Sinai area for the use of troops. In December, he, Newcombe and Woolley were posted to the Army's Information Service in Cairo. Lawrence's job was to draw maps, to interrogate Turkish prisoners in order to pinpoint the distribution of Turkish troops and to draw up a manual for the use of officers on active duty.

Lawrence took a perverse pleasure in shocking and antagonizing the professional soldiers by refusing to dress in complete uniform, riding the biggest and noisiest motor-cycle he could find, rewriting official reports, correcting their grammar and exasperating his superiors in every possible way. Because of this impish behaviour he was considered an upstart by most of the staff of British G.H.Q. whose standards of discipline and training were continually outraged by his disregard for rank and disrespect for authority.

❖   ❖   ❖

At this point in time the Ottoman empire of Turkey held sway over virtually the whole of the Arabian peninsula, including the now independent nations,

Iraq, Syria, Lebanon, Israel, Jordan, Saudi Arabia and Yemen. But secret Arab societies in Mesopotamia and Syria, known as the Ahab and the Fetah, were preparing for the day when a general Arab uprising against their Turkish masters might prove opportune. Among the leading spirits in this fermenting rebellion were the Grand Sherif of Mecca, Hussein, and his four sons, Ali, Abdulla, Feisal and Zeid.

Hussein was a direct descendant of the Prophet Mohammed and was the head of the Dhawi Aun section of the Hashemite family, which took its name from Hashem, a distinguished tribal leader of the seventh century and the great-grandfather of the Prophet. Ever since the time of Mohammed, a member of the Prophet's family had been Emir of Mecca and, after the Turks had imposed their rule upon the Holy Places of Islam in the Hejaz—Mecca and Medina—they continued the custom, although the Emir was from then on subject to the orders of Constantinople.

Shortly before the revolution of the Young Turks in 1911 which ousted the Sultan, Abdul Hamid, certain members of the Hashemite family were removed on the Sultan's orders to "honourable captivity" in Constantinople. Among them were Hussein and his four sons, who at their father's wise insistence profited from the experience by gaining a modern education, which afterwards greatly helped them to lead the Arab armies to victory. Then, with the advent of the Young Turks, Hussein was sent back to Mecca as Emir.

When war broke out in 1914 the Turks, partly impelled by their desire to recover their former North African domains now under British and French control, decided to invite the Arabs to join in a *Jehad,* or Holy War, to drive the Christian infidels from all Islamic lands. The key lay in getting the co-operation of Mecca. But Hussein was unwilling to be drawn into the venture, seeing that behind the pretence of a struggle for Islamic unity lay the design to strengthen Turkey's hold over its dominions. In any case he felt that a Holy War declared by Turkey with a Christian ally, Germany, was absurd and would end in a bloodbath with no profit and much loss to the Arabs. Besides, he was himself preparing, in concert with the Ahab and Fetah, for a revolt against the Turks and had since before the war been seeking British aid to this end. But, when the Turks approached him in 1915, he deemed it prudent to appear to play along with them and sent Feisal to Damascus to discuss the Turkish plan as his representative and, secretly, to report to him on the possibilities of the Syrians joining an Arab revolt. At the same time he sent Ali to Medina to raise discreetly an Arab army from the local villagers and Hejazi tribesmen and Abdulla to Cairo to negotiate for British support.

But these were anxious days for Britain and by no means encouraging for an Arab success. The British frontal assault on the Dardanelles had been repulsed with heavy losses on both sides; British forces, trying a back-door entry to Turkey's domains through Mesopotamia, were besieged at Kut on the Tigris; and the Senussi tribes in the Libyan desert were threatening Britain's rear in Egypt. Still the Grand Sherif, in that blind way of his that was ten years later to prove his undoing at the hands of Ibn Saud, went ahead with his plans for an Arab uprising. Feisal, a virtual prisoner in Damascus whose every move was carefully watched by the Turks, was in a most hazardous position. Syria was in no state to rebel. Cowed beneath the merciless brutalities of its Turkish Governor, Jemal Pasha, those of its leaders who had not been executed were in hiding and its peasantry were being conscripted into Turkish army units. Feisal wrote to his father to counsel delay at least until the tide of war between Britain and Turkey might change.

1

On the morning of the first day of June in 1916, a public execution was about to take place in Damascus. As the first light of the dawn cast its pale streaks across the city's main square, the ragged figure of an Arab, that had once been a man but was now a tortured bleeding wretch, was led out to face his executioner. In the middle of the square stood a rough-hewn gibbet. A thin coil of rope dangled from the horizontal and an army mule-cart was backed against the upright. The method of execution was simple and barbaric. The prisoner was frog-marched onto the cart, the hangman placed the noose around his neck and a moment later the cart would be dragged away, leaving the victim to throttle to death, or, if his struggles should be so prolonged as to threaten the timetable and postpone the Governor's breakfast, until the hangman gave a tug at his legs and broke his spinal cord.

On a platform separated from the crowd a group of men watched the executions. Seven of them were Turks—the Governor of Syria, Jemal Pasha, the prison commandant and their aides-de-camp. The eighth was an Arab, slight of face and body, with deep-set dark eyes, long thin nose and sensitive mouth encompassed by a well trimmed and pointed black beard. Despite his lack of height the Emir Feisal looked every inch a son of the Sherif of Mecca, a prince of Arabia and lord of the desert, betraying no marks of his long captivity as the "guest" of Jemal Pasha and outwardly unmoved by the insults and indignities to his race with which his hosts delighted to taunt him.

The men about to be hanged that morning were another group of his Syrian friends whom the Turks had accused of plotting against the Ottoman Empire, dangerous revolutionaries fired by the ideal of Arab freedom. One of them was a cousin of his, with whom he had been meeting secretly until a few weeks before his arrest. For some time it had been Jemal's custom to force Feisal to witness these executions in the hope that the Emir's physical presence at the Governor's side would discourage other rebels by suggesting that he had sold out to the Turks or would provoke an outburst from one of the doomed men, which would incriminate him as the real leader of the Arab nationalists in Syria. But not one of those condemned had shown any sign of recognizing Feisal, nor he of them. Both he and they knew that the smallest sign of mutual recognition would have revealed what the hated Turks wished to discover and so have destroyed their hope of Arab freedom.

So, while his fellow conspirators dangled in death at the end of a Turkish rope, Feisal had always stood upon Jemal's platform with eyes unseeing and impassive concealing the cold fury in his heart—always, that is, except for one occasion when his temper got the better of his self-control. A boy no more than twelve years old and the son of a close friend had been caught carrying a message to Mecca from the Fetah. Being only a very light weight the boy's death struggles were unusually prolonged. Also he was the last of his group to hang and therefore unlikely to delay the Governor's lavish breakfast. As the platform party turned to go, leaving the boy slowly to throttle himself, Feisal lashed out at Jemal.

"This brutality will cost you everything you are trying to avoid. Your Turkish justice will be avenged."

"Treasonable talk such as that from one who wears the uniform of a Turkish officer is punishable by death," Jemal Pasha retorted coldly.

Feisal was thereupon arrested and spent the next few weeks in solitary confinement, never knowing when he might be taken out and hanged. But, after wiser counsels in Constantinople had decided that he was more valuable to the Turks alive than dead, orders came to release him from prison and he became once more the so-called guest of Jemal Pasha. His near escape from death was not without its effect upon his nerves. Added to this, the war news which he received on his release could scarcely have been more gloomy. The Allied plan for landing at Alexandretta to drive a wedge between Turkey and her Arabian empire had been abandoned, the Dardanelles operation had proved a costly failure and British forces were about to surrender at Kut—the only real toe-hold they had obtained within Turkish occupied territory. Inside Syria, the hope of a national uprising was waning under the ruthless repressions of Jemal.

Feisal knew of the preparations for revolt in the Hejaz which his father Sherif Hussein and his brother Ali were undertaking under the guise of gathering together a force to help the Turks' plans for a Holy War. But from his captivity in Damascus, where week after week he had to watch the destruction of his hopes and the death and torture of his friends, he came increasingly to doubt the possibilities of any revolt in Syria and to fear for the consequences of a rising in the Hejaz upon himself and the few Arab leaders whom the Turks had not yet destroyed.

Once he had made a bid to escape to Medina on the pretext that he had been requested to inspect the Arab forces there before they left to join in the Turkish attack on Egypt. But his plan was forestalled by Jemal, who insisted on accompanying him on his journey and also taking along the Turkish Commander-in-Chief, General Enver Pasha. While the Arab cavalry and camel corps were going through their battle exercises, some of the Sheikhs suggested in a whispered aside to Feisal that they should kill the two Turks there and then and raise the crimson flag of the Grand Sherif in proclamation of the Arab revolt. But Feisal, inhibited by Arab codes and customs, had refused. "We cannot kill them, they are our guests."

The Sheikhs had protested that this was carrying custom too far. "You would spare the lives of those who have murdered your own friends before your eyes." But Feisal stood firm, even to the point of placing his guests under the escort of his own slaves and accompanying them back to Damascus. "There are more honourable ways of raising the standard of Arab freedom than by violating sacred Arab codes," he told his friends as he took his leave for the journey back to Syria.

Back in Damascus the Turks, not satisfied by the Hashemite protestations of loyalty that had been offered to them in the Hejaz, decided to reinforce their garrison at Medina. Towards Feisal, however, they showed their gratitude for his protection by relaxing the strict control which they had placed on his movements since his release from prison. Yet Feisal still feared to make any sudden move. The war news was no better; the British in Egypt were licking their wounds from the Dardanelles and Kut; and now Medina was full of Turkish troops under the butcher of Armenia, Fakhri Pasha, which seemed to neutralize the only possible area for an organized rising.

Feisal wrote regularly to his father counselling restraint. Hussein replied equally regularly that he could not wait much longer. Then, on the day of the execution of Feisal's cousin, a message came from Mecca. The Grand Sherif could wait no longer. Four days from the despatch of this notice the Arab revolt would be proclaimed in Mecca. Feisal must escape with all speed and join his family in the Hejaz. . . . "*Insh'allah,* we shall soon be free." The Emir knew from his father's tone that it was useless to argue further the wisdom of delay. The hour was about to strike and he must strike with it. Heaven only knew just where and how, but of one thing there could be no doubt—in a few days' time Damascus was going to be a most unhealthy place for a son of Hussein.

Two nights later Feisal left his quarters and, accompanied by a small retinue of friends and servants, rode out into the Syrian desert to a pre-arranged meeting with Nuri Shaalan, the Paramount Chief of the Ruwalla tribe. Escorted by Nuri's Bedouins he then made for Mecca under the blood-red banner of his father; and, as he rode out into the desert, a new lightness of heart seemed to overcome his earlier doubts and torments. The die was cast. The decision that he could not make had made itself. He was committed now to a single, simple purpose—victory, the unity and independence of Arabia and the cleansing of its soil of foreign oppression.

2

The news of the Arab Revolt in the Hejaz and of Feisal's escape from Damascus was received with surprising coldness by British G.H.Q. in Egypt. At the outset the Arabs, profiting from the advantage of surprise, had succeeded in taking Mecca, Jidda, Yenbo and Rabegh—the last three, useful ports on the Red Sea. But they were unable to keep up this momentum for very long and the attack on Medina was repulsed with severe losses to Ali's and Feisal's troops in lives and morale.

The reverse strengthened the view of General Archibald Murray, then British Commander-in-Chief in the Middle East, and of his staff, that the Arabs' fighting potentialities were too low to be worth the subsidies that Britain had started to pay from the moment the Sherif raised his flag of revolt. "Just a rabble, old man. No trained officers, no knowledge of tactics or strategy. A motley crew of camel stealers, no match for the well-seasoned Turk." These and other similar epithets were common coin in the offices and messes at headquarters, convenient phrases to dismiss the idea of an Arab uprising and with it the need to do any rethinking of campaign strategy.

Only a small handful of young officers thought otherwise. Ronald Storrs, Oriental Secretary to the British Residency in Cairo and later to become Governor of Jerusalem, a brilliant young diplomat, expert in the affairs of the Middle East and a man of the finest intellect, was the most senior amongst them. Then there was George Lloyd, who became

Lord Lloyd and a distinguished British Cabinet Minister, and Colonel Clayton, the Chief of Intelligence, who had the wisdom and calm courage to take a view broader than the military. Most junior of all the supporters of the Arab Revolt was T. E. Lawrence, then serving as a junior officer in the Maps Division of G.H.Q.

When the news first broke about Hussein's rising against the Turks, Lawrence's impatience knew no bounds. Desperate to get away from his office stool, he yearned to be able to join the Arab armies. Openly aggressive to the sceptics at G.H.Q. who decried the value of Hussein's movement, he became more and more unpopular with his superiors and unsociable towards his equals, particularly as the news of the Arab revolt and the interpretations of G.H.Q. began to suggest that the whole rebellion might peter out in a few weeks and the Grand Sherif would end by choking to death on a Turkish gallows. Lawrence bitterly retorted that any set-backs were due to a total absence of liaison between the Arab forces and the British, to a lack of proper military information about the strength and dispositions of the enemy and to the absolute failure of British headquarters to give enough material help. By these and other thrusts and taunts at his superiors, Lawrence, not altogether without design, brought the thermometer of his relationships at G.H.Q. to boiling point, so that when he heard that Storrs was going to visit Abdulla at Jidda to discuss future plans he had no difficulty in getting ten days' leave to go along "for the joyride," as he put it. G.H.Q. were thankful to get rid of this argumentative and opinionated associate. Had they known his real purpose and how deeply he intended to involve himself and them too in the destiny of the Arab revolt, they might not have parted from him so casually. But, not for the last time, Lawrence concealed his true intentions from his superiors. In his own words, "Storrs and I then marched off together, happily. In the East they swore that by three sides was the decent way across a square; and my trick to escape was in this sense oriental. But I justified myself by my confidence in the final success of the Arab revolt if properly advised. I had been a mover in its beginning; my hopes lay in it. . . ."

Lawrence had already started to dream of writing his own page of history. As his ship sailed out of Suez he resolved that somewhere in Arabia he would find the Prophet and leader of the Arab Revolt and, having found him, guide him to their joint destiny in Damascus.

❖   ❖   ❖

This strange little party of reconnaissance was met at Jidda by a launch sent by the British representative to the infant Arab State, Colonel Wilson, a stiff and downright type who had little in common with the artistic sense of Storrs and the youthful ebullience of Lawrence. Wilson, ignoring in his businesslike British way the paralysing heat of the Red Sea's noonday, arranged an immediate interview with the Emir Abdulla, Foreign Minister of the Arab State by paternal appointment.

To Lawrence's surprise, Abdulla arrived in the best of cheer, apparently unabashed by the stalemate into which the Arab revolt had run after only a few months. At first Lawrence put this down to mere delight at meeting Storrs once again, an old friend with whom he had conducted business for some time past. But the merriment that rippled around Abdulla's fat cheeks and short pursed lips and his easy jesting manner with all about him persisted beyond the opening courtesies and pleasantries and disappointed Lawrence in its persistence.

Eventually Storrs managed to work the conversation round to serious matters, asking for the Emir's views on the state of the Arab revolt. Abdulla's expression became more serious and he chose his words carefully, as he sought to explain the Arabs' failure to capture Medina. The Turks had been allowed to reinforce with men and supplies because the British had neglected to cut the Hejaz railway. General Wingate, who headed the British military liaison staff with Sherif Hussein, had landed some troops at Rabegh for the defence of Mecca, but had failed not only to cut the enemy's supply line but also to supply arms and ammunition to the Arabs. The Harb, one of the biggest local tribes, had defected to the Turks out of disbelief that they would gain anything from rebellion. Worst of all the Turks were massing for a breakout from Medina to recapture Mecca. To avert such a disaster Abdulla asked for a British brigade to prepare to rush to Rabegh directly the Turks broke out of Medina. Lawrence interjected that the British forces in Egypt were short of troops and even more of shipping to transport them on such a venture. He also reminded Abdulla that his own father had asked that the Hejaz railway should not be sabotaged as he wished to use it for his own later advance on Damascus.

This one meeting with Abdulla convinced Lawrence that here was no leader of the Arab revolt. Though only thirty-five years old, the Emir seemed to lack the vitality that would breathe fire into the Arab heart; he was too shrewd, too comfortable, too much inclined to humour and too good a talker to be able or willing to demand of himself or his men that effort that stretched up to and even beyond the limits of endurance.

Such were the qualities of leadership that Lawrence sought. Without a man capable of giving this much to the cause he doubted that the Arab awakening could survive the trials and torments that lay ahead of it and feared it would wither and die a still-born child for lack of a willingness to sacrifice all on the part of those who had given it birth. As they argued on into the burning afternoon, Lawrence became increasingly obsessed with the idea of seeking out Feisal and testing him for the rôle of the new prophet of

Arabia. Abdulla, shrewdly sensing what this impatient young Englishman was after and not a little relieved that he had clearly been rejected for the part, readily agreed to support Lawrence's request for permission to visit his brother.

Taking the telephone in his podgy hands he spoke to his father in Mecca. But the old man was not at all enthusiastic. Abdulla argued, but to no avail. Hussein was highly suspicious. What was Lawrence's purpose? He did not trust these English infidels. All right to have them in Jidda where they could be carefully watched, but to let them wander about the desert peering into things that were not their business would be another and altogether more dangerous thing. Abdulla then handed over to Storrs, who turned on his fullest diplomatic charm and—though not without some difficulty—managed to persuade the Sherif of Mecca that Lawrence would conduct himself as a friend and not as a spy and that as a friend all that he wanted to do was to discover how best the British could supply Feisal's needs and support his plans for the campaign against the Turks. Softened by these assurances and attracted by the hope of British arms for his Bedouins, Hussein instructed Abdulla to see to it that Lawrence was conducted safely to Feisal's camp in the desert hills about Medina.

3

Feisal's headquarters were then at Wadi Safra about two hundred miles north of Jidda and some sixty miles south-west of Medina. It was agreed that in the interest of speed the first half of the journey should be by ship as far as Rabegh where the Emir Ali, the eldest of Hussein's sons and the local commander, should provide the necessary camels for Lawrence and his escort.

The evening before his departure Lawrence received further confirmation of his belief in Feisal as opposed to Abdulla. Colonel Wilson had invited the Emir to a dinner at his house, an odd occasion graced by Abdulla, Storrs and Lawrence with an Egyptian general, Sayed Ali, and the Chief of Staff of Hussein's Arab army, Aziz el Misri, who had previously led the Turkish forces against the Italians and later headed a revolt of Arab officers in the Turkish army. Abdulla brought along his band, a ragged collection of Turkish musicians whom the Sherifian forces had captured with the Turkish Governor-General at Taif near Mecca at the outset of the revolt. Laughing delightedly at the discordant and mournful noises emitted by his unhappy captives, Abdulla told Storrs and Lawrence of how he had planned the Arab revolt. His idea had been to seize a group of leading Moslem pilgrims to Mecca. These would have included the ruling men of Turkey as well as important leaders from India and Egypt. With these hostages he would have sought to pressure Constantinople both directly and indirectly through Delhi and Cairo to

concede the demands of the Sherif of Mecca in return
for the release of their subjects. But Feisal had spoilt
his clever trick by persuading their father to have
nothing to do with it. Lawrence agreed with Feisal
that liberty was something that must be fought for
and not negotiated by blackmail.

At Rabegh Lawrence met Ali and took an immediate liking to this sad and sallow young man
whose only similarity to his brothers lay in the fact
that he too looked older than his years. Lawrence
found him very much a creature after his own heart,
an intellectual in a wilderness of illiteracy, thoroughly
well read in law and religion, honest and direct to the
point that he failed to see dishonesty in others, a far
cry from his brother Abdulla, whom Lawrence had
just left to brood upon his conspiracies in Jidda. Ali's
main shortcoming was purely physical. He was a
consumptive and this weakness had left him with a
certain nervousness and lassitude which he found difficult to overcome except in periodic moments of
violent passion which were usually followed by bouts
of mulish obstinacy.

Ali was far from enthusiastic about Lawrence's
plan but accepted his father's orders with a good
grace. He insisted that Lawrence should not start until
after sunset so that the expedition should be kept secret, even from his own slaves, and he enjoined upon
the escort to avoid meeting with anyone or visiting
any camps on the journey. The tribes in the neighbourhood of Rabegh were Masruh Harb and owed allegiance to Hussein Mabeirig who, according to
Abdulla's tale of woe in Jidda which Ali confirmed,
had joined the Turks. Ali feared that if word got to
Mabeirig of Lawrence's journey to Feisal he would
be waylaid. His father would then hold him, Ali, responsible for whatever fate might befall their English
guest, for, although it would have been fully within
the code of an Arab and the faith of a Moslem to
kill an infidel who trespassed upon his ground, once
the infidel had been accepted as a guest his hosts

must answer for his deliverance in safety to his destination. For good measure Ali appointed a guide called Tafas as his bodyguard. Tafas was of the Beni Salem tribe who were feuding with the Masruh, which fact inclined the grizzled old warrior towards his English charge.

Two nights and two days later Lawrence and his escort reached Hamra in the Wadi Safra. At the approaches to the village the rock-walled valley teemed with Feisal's soldiers, their bivouacs nestling together in every available patch of shade, their hobbled riding camels clumsily searching out every edible clump of greenery that clung precariously to life among the stone-grey hills. Across a stream and along a track lined by walls on either side like a trench with defensive parapets, they came to the doorway of a long single-storeyed house. There as in an oil painting stood Feisal, waiting to receive this strange young visitor, his white robes and slender figure making him seem taller by inches, his hands resting on the gold dagger in his waistband—token of his Sherifian rank—a statue immobile in every detail save for the ever watchful, piercing eyes, black beads darting like quicksilver, the unslumbering sentinels of a desert prince. Here in this first magnetic moment of meeting was the man whom he had come to find—the prophet of the Arab awakening.

Lawrence could not contain his excitement over his discovery. As Feisal motioned him to his reception room, dark as an underground vault with the shutters locked against the furnace heat of the sun, his whole body trembled with excitement and it seemed that the brief preliminary courtesies and compliments would never end. Feisal enquired about the journey, commenting that Lawrence had covered the ground with remarkable speed considering that this was his first experience of camel riding. Then silence, broken only by the pinging of a mosquito and the muffled slapping of Arab hands upon bearded cheeks. Feisal looked about him at the solemn faces of his retinue, cross-legged on the plushy carpets that covered the simple stone floor, inviting them with the lift of an eyebrow to speak out and question their English guest, whose restless blue eyes and taut drawn mouth betrayed an uncontrollable impetuosity. But nobody spoke and the tensed air seemed to stretch between them like a rubber band, quivering silently and drawing all eyes to the inevitable moment of breaking. Then, very softly, Feisal spoke yet another introduction, asking how his visitor liked this place in the hills.

The rubber band had reached breaking point. The restless eyes wheeled suddenly and fixed in a fierce stare as if to penetrate the heavy wooden shutters on the windows, the taut lips parted and almost in a shout Lawrence burst out, "Well; but it is far from Damascus."

4

Feisal, thoroughly depressed and tired by his recent retreat from Medina, was in no mood to follow this ambitious line of talk and decided to prick the bubble of Lawrence's exuberance. With a laugh that was almost a sigh he replied, "There are plenty of Turks to fight a lot nearer to us than Damascus."

The tension snapped as the cross-legged company laughed with their leader and Lawrence flushed with the embarrassment of the amateur who has spoken out of turn to a group of professionals. Feisal turned towards his guest and, with a warm smile suddenly softening the grave expression of his eyes, he asked Lawrence to explain his mission. Lawrence replied that he had come to enquire how the Arab revolt was progressing, what were its requirements and what were Feisal's plans for future action against the Turks. He would report on his findings to Cairo where the Arabs' new-found allies waited anxiously for news and stood ready to help in every way possible.

"Were you sent by British headquarters?" asked Maulud el Mukhlus, Feisal's A.D.C. and a former commander of Turkish cavalry who had been one of the first Arab officers to leave the Ottoman army and join Sherif Hussein's rebellion.

"Nobody sent me," Lawrence candidly replied. "I came myself, first to Jidda, and now by order of the Sherif of Mecca to Feisal." Then with a sly dig at Abdulla which he saw by Feisal's fleeting half smile was not lost on the Emir, "I wanted to be able to convey a first-hand report from those who are doing the fighting."

"So you have no authority, yet you ask to know everything of our plans and prospects," said a surly voice, which Lawrence recognized as bearing a strong Syrian accent. "My belief is that you have come as a spy."

"I come to you as a friend who will plead your cause in high places in Cairo," Lawrence retorted, looking directly at his Syrian accuser. "I come to help you avenge the murders of your Syrian brothers on the scaffolds of Damascus."

"Bah! Those men were but British and French agents; no friends of the Arabs, for they were ready to sell their country to your rulers, just as you would have us do with your talk of British help. We should send him away, my lord, before he finds out even more than he must know already about our situation."

Feisal smiled. "You see," he said to Lawrence, "our alliance with Britain is yet but a matter of convenience. We are still too jealous for our lands to trust any outside power as friend to friend. Maybe it will be different one day——"

"No, never," the Syrian interrupted. "Is it not all too clear? This talk of Damascus. 'We are far from Damascus, we must help you to avenge the murders of Damascus.' Why does this stranger speak so much of our capital, if he is not trying to find out our plans for taking it so that he and his English friends can get there first?"

Lawrence tried to reason logically with this implacable adversary. "I well understand your suspicions of me and my countrymen. Yet the only way I can disarm these suspicions is by coming to you and proving that I am your friend and ally. There are today thousands of British soldiers in France but the French people do not suspect Britain of trying to annex their country. Why then should the Arabs fear being taken over merely because Britain and Britishers who come among you offer their help to evict the Turks?"

"I am jealous for the Hejaz," Feisal replied. "And though I know the British do not want it, yet what can I say, when they took the Sudan, also not wanting it? They hunger for desolate lands, to build them up; and so, perhaps one day Arabia will seem to them precious. Your good and my good, perhaps they are different, and either forced good or forced evil will make a people cry with pain. Does the ore admire the flame which transforms it? There is no reason 'for offence, but a people too weak are clamant over their little own. Our race will have a cripple's temper till it has found its feet."

Realizing that Feisal intended this speech to end the argument, Lawrence rose and excused himself. He had learnt more in these last few minutes about the sensitivities of the Arabs than in all his earlier studies. Britain was not going to buy their friendship with a handful of gold and a shipload of arms, as most people seemed to think back at G.H.Q. It would take a lot of time and patience to win their confidence and patience with Arabs was not in plentiful supply in Cairo. Also nobody at headquarters would be the least bit interested by a mere disquisition from a young captain on the importance of overcoming Arab suspicions unless it were accompanied at least by detailed information of Feisal's future plans and, best of all, by some proof of his army's ability to take on and beat the Turks. Lawrence decided that he must tackle Feisal, if possible, alone. The Emir's manner towards him during the debate just ended had suggested that winning his confidence might not be an altogether insuperable problem. Although he had adopted his traditional tribal rôle of umpire, he had seemed more anxious to explain matters to his guest than to heckle him. This could, of course, have been mere Arab courtesy. Yet somehow Lawrence mused to himself, "he seemed to like me," and with a self-satisfied grunt lay down to sleep off the exhaustion that now overcame him.

❖   ❖   ❖

The next day Feisal invited Lawrence to make a tour of inspection of his troops. Their first call was with the Egyptian detachment which had been sent from the Sudan by General Wingate. They included a battery of mountain artillery and a machine-gun unit. Lawrence commented upon their equipment and Feisal smiled a knowing smile at Maulud.

"They arrived too late," he said.

"Too late for what?"

"To capture Medina," Feisal replied, his voice suddenly harsh. The smile vanished and his lips set in a thin hard line. "Tell him, Maulud."

Maulud began to pour out the bitter story of their attempt to take Medina. The Turks had been superior in every way. It was like pitting dervishes against trained troops. The Arab army was short of everything—of food, money and arms. They had no guns, not even machine-guns, not enough rifles to go round and a hopelessly inadequate supply of ammunition.

Feisal then took up the refrain. It had been a terrible experience, with raw unseasoned troops outnumbered and outgunned. Owing to a total lack of intelligence, the attack was timed for the moment when not only had Fakhri Pasha's reinforcements just settled in, but an extra force had arrived on its way to the Yemen. After the first wave of the attack had been repulsed, the Turks had opened up with their artillery on the retreating tribesmen who broke in blind and ignorant panic, having never before been subjected to this kind of bombardment. All his and Ali's efforts to rally their troops had failed and at length in desperation they had called off the assault. Worse still was the retribution meted out by Fakhri to a group of Beni Salem tribesmen who offered to surrender in the hope of saving their villages. In reply

Fakhri had surrounded them and massacred every man, woman and child.

This terrible act of butchery had been received with horror throughout all Arabia, where the codes of war held that women and children were inviolate. The Arab peoples now knew beyond any doubt that there could be no compromise with such enemies. But sheer fury and avenging fervour were not enough to defeat the well-trained Turks nor to rally the tribes to active rebellion. The Arab army must have guns, field and mountain pieces, and guns with a range at least equal to the enemy's artillery. The Egyptian guns had looked good and made a loud noise, which had at first helped morale, but in a recent encounter with a Turkish advance column the enemy's guns had proved to have twice the range and had been able to force yet another retreat upon the Arabs.

Feisal had asked Ali to go to Rabegh to enquire why no supplies were coming forward and his brother's report had all but made him and his followers throw in their hand. Ali had found that most of the materials sent from Egypt had been stolen by Hussein Mabeirig's dissident tribesmen, whereupon the supply had been stopped.

Still, if the British would only send some guns, plus of course enough small arms and ammunition, Feisal said that he would regroup his army for another attempt at Medina. His plan was to attack with his eight thousand tribesmen from the west, while Ali moved up from Rabegh with three thousand regular Arab infantry, and Zeid, their nineteen-year-old half brother, led a diversionary attack against the Turkish force at Bir Abbas to stop them moving to the relief of the Medina garrison. Abdulla would come in from the east with an army of four thousand, thus surrounding the Turks on virtually all sides. Even if this attack should fail to carry Medina it would at least deal a heavy blow at Turkish preparations against Mecca and so give the Sherif's armies time to make ready for further operations.

As Feisal came to the end of his exposition with a final *"Insh'allah,"* Lawrence noticed that, though he still looked physically worn, his spirit seemed to have been uplifted by the mere recital of the plans for battle; and his smile, as Maulud fiercely drove home once again the need for mountain guns to blast the Turks to fragments, left no doubt that he had been made glad, and hopeful, by this unexpected visitation. Gone was the mood of ill-concealed despair of the previous night. As he rose to take his leave and attend to his prayers, a shaft of sunlight caught the gold and scarlet cords of his headdress transforming it for a fleeting moment into a jewelled crown. "The King of all Arabia, crowned in Damascus," Lawrence thought to himself, "and I the Kingmaker."

5

Before leaving to report his findings to G.H.Q. Lawrence made a brief reconnaissance of the terrain between Feisal's mountain camp and the Turkish-occupied plains that stretched eastwards to Medina. He also sought out groups of Feisal's soldiers to test their reactions to their situation. The men he found in good heart, not least because as soldiers they were being more handsomely paid than ever before and their families were being fed as well by the Sherif's bounty. Typically of their race, these simple men from the desert hills were unconcerned with the future and its problems and dangers. Good and solid defensive material, Lawrence thought, who with some modern machine-guns could be depended upon to hold the rugged mountain passes that lay between the Turks and Mecca, but not the type to carry forward an offensive against a well-trained and securely entrenched enemy.

Arrived at Jidda, Lawrence discovered that General Wingate, to whom he must make his report as the man in command of British troops in Arabia, was then in Khartoum. Admiral Wemyss, British Naval Commander in Egypt, was on his way to confer with his army colleague and, being himself of that small band of believers in the Arab revolt, he readily agreed to take Lawrence along with him. His only condition was to insist that Lawrence change into his proper British uniform and not appear on his quarter-deck in an Arab fancy-dress, as he termed the robes which, though he no longer needed to appear as an Arab for his own safety, Lawrence had persisted in wearing while travelling from Rabegh to Jidda in a ship of the Royal Navy. Lawrence explained this affectation as being necessary to help him to identify himself with the Arabs; but the lengths to which he carried it in non-Arab company, in Cairo and even after the war at the Paris Peace Conference, suggest that he also could not resist the urge to show off and appear as the centre of attraction.

In Khartoum Wingate was relieved to hear of Feisal's plans for a fresh assault on Medina. Like Wemyss, he had not subscribed to the jaundiced views of the staff in Cairo about the chances of Hussein's rebellion. But, a simple honest soldier, with little political sense, he failed to appreciate that Arab sensitivities about the presence of large numbers of European troops must be taken into account. His idea was to send a strong force of British and French troops to the Hejaz to help Feisal to polish off the Turks and then with this same force to push on northwards alongside the main British armies into Syria. In this he had been much encouraged by the wily French representative in Jidda, Colonel Bremond, whose policy was to win Syria for France—and no doubt its governorship for Colonel Bremond—while pretending to the Arabs that the Anglo-French forces were merely there to help them regain their freedom and their lands.

Lawrence was fully alive to Bremond's designs. They had met in Jidda and taken an immediate dislike to each other. He therefore argued all the more fiercely with Wingate that to send a large force of Europeans to Arabia would defeat its object and result in the Arab tribes deserting to their homes and abandoning the struggle. On the other hand, Feisal desperately needed money, guns and food, plus a small group of British officers to instruct the Bedouin in the use of modern weapons. With such help he could hold the mountains for an indefinite period.

Wingate, although surprised and even a little

shocked by the vehemence of this young officer, that
bordered on arrogance, in the face of his superiors,
was not moved by his arguments. This, the General
considered, was altogether too passive a concept and
too defensive a strategy for the Arab revolt, and forthwith decided to telegraph to G.H.Q. to recommend
the immediate dispatch of several large Allied con-
tingents to the Hejaz. Lawrence, deeply dismayed,
pondered on what he should do next. Only action in
Cairo could, it seemed, now prevent the well-inten-
tioned rashness of Wingate being translated into an
act of folly which would sour British relations with
the Arabs and destroy all hope of effective co-operation with their movement. He therefore hastened to
G.H.Q. to plead his case and demand an interview
with no less a figure than Sir Archibald Murray, the
British Commander-in-Chief.

To his great surprise, he found a reasonably warm
welcome awaiting him. He soon discovered that his
new-found popularity was due to the report that he
had sent to Colonel Clayton violently disputing Wingate's recommendations for an Allied landing on the
Arabian coast. G.H.Q. were in no mood to spare
troops for such a venture and it was in any case unlikely that they would get authority to do so from
London, where the new government of Mr. Lloyd
George—never a great partisan of the Arab cause—
was preoccupied with the stalemate and the slaughter
of the Western front in Europe. The report from a
"man-on-the-spot" arguing so strongly against the
use of British or French troops in Arabia therefore
came as most welcome ammunition to counter Wingate's highly inconvenient and over-enthusiastic proposals. Lawrence, realizing the importance of this unexpected alliance with headquarters, used it with skill
in dealing with Murray and his Chief of Staff, General
Lyndon Bell, who readily agreed to the alternative
compromise of sending the Arabs the supplies and
the instructors they needed and ordered Lawrence to

return to the Hejaz as liaison officer with Feisal's army.

Lawrence went through the motions of protesting his unsuitability for the assignment. His trade was not that of a fighting soldier, he said, but rather of a man of books, who disliked responsibility and had no aptitude for the military profession. But he was careful not to protest too strongly and, when Clayton insisted that he must go, he almost rushed out of the room. His heart was swelling with that impetuous throb which only those know who are about to fulfil some overpowering secret ambition. He could now return to the Arab armies no longer having to confess himself a private adventurer; he was now the envoy and emissary of the British command in Egypt, appointed to guide Feisal and the Arab revolt towards the goal of Damascus. The self-styled kingmaker had been confirmed in his commission.

Yet even at this early stage the kingmaker was not without his doubts as to the prospects of securing the throne of Arabia for his chosen lord. During his stay in Cairo Lawrence had got to hear of the Sykes-Picot agreement. This was a secret arrangement between Britain and France, which in theory provided that, after the Ottoman empire had been destroyed, independent Arab states should be set up and based on Damascus, Aleppo and Mosul. In practice, however, its purpose was to secure the post-war carve up of Arabia between Britain, France and Russia for the establishment of Allied Protectorates from the Mediterranean to the Indian Ocean. These arrangements were in complete contradiction of the pledges which Kitchener's successor in Egypt, Sir Henry McMahon, had given to the Grand Sherif before the start of the Arab revolt and which the Sherif, his family, and his followers, as Lawrence had discovered in his talks with Abdulla and Feisal, interpreted as promising freedom and unity to all Arabia, once the Turks had been driven out.

❖   ❖   ❖

Early in November Lawrence returned to Yenbo, a small peninsular port built on a coral reef in the Red Sea north of Rabegh. Here his first forebodings of Allied intentions were to be supplemented by a severe jolt to his belief in the effectiveness of the Arabs. To his dismay he found the place full of Feisal's soldiers who had retreated there after another defeat by the Turks. The enemy had anticipated the Arab plan of attack on Medina and had struck first to break through to the coast and prevent the armies of the Sherif's four sons joining up for the assault. Feisal had been beaten back to Yenbo, Zeid had been all but captured, Ali's advance from Rabegh to join forces with Feisal had been broken up by a Turkish counter-attack, and Abdulla had hardly got started from Mecca. The atmosphere in the town was not far short of panic and the only reassurance in sight was the grey wall of British warships moored in the little harbour—reinforcements sent by Wemyss on hearing of the latest Arab rout.

Each of the Sherif's sons was convinced that he had been let down by the intrigues of his brothers. Ali had returned, embittered and ill, to Rabegh muttering threats to quit the struggle altogether. Worse still, Lawrence discovered that many of the Arab forces had deserted, taking their rifles with them. And all this had happened since the first shiploads of fresh arms and ammunition, including five-inch howitzer guns, had reached Arabia, as well as a group of British instructors.

Lawrence set off in search of Feisal, feeling deeply disillusioned. Were the Arabs so hopeless that they could not even defend their own hills with modern equipment? Was his mission on their behalf to end thus in an ignominious retreat into the sea? But Feisal was surprisingly cheerful in face of these reverses. Too many wild rumours were rife among his army, he explained. True, one of the Harb tribes had gone over to the enemy but this did not signal the end of Arab resistance. More than ever he was trying to restore the morale of his forces, making himself available to his tribesmen, listening to their smallest complaints and disputes and countering the defeatist talk that was going the rounds of the camp. Lawrence set to work to help Feisal to encourage his troops and for several days the two of them hardly slept at all in their efforts to talk the frightened Bedouins into a more robust attitude of mind.

The daylight hours were spent in inspections of men and equipment, supervising the digging of defensive positions and visiting the classes held by the British instructors in the use of small arms and high explosives. At night Feisal's tent resembled more a market square than a place of rest, with callers coming and going in a constant stream—but going, so Lawrence noticed, a great deal more confident than they came. At intervals during the night they would eat a meal of dates and some spiced cakes, sent by Feisal's Circassian grandmother from Mecca, and wash it down with the bitter Arab coffee that quenches the thirst of the desert like no other liquid. After an hour or two of rest they would rise with the cold dawn and be off again upon their rounds. Although at times exhausted by lack of sleep Lawrence kept at his task, knowing that, if Feisal could go this pace and drive himself this hard, he must on no account fall short for fear of losing the respect of his Arab brothers-in-arms.

As was generally expected, the Turks did not wait long before staging their final attack to drive Feisal into the sea. At eleven o'clock one night the alarm sounded. The Arab outposts had reported three enemy battalions to be three miles away from Yenbo and advancing on the town. The garrison went quietly and in good military order to its appointed defensive posts. There was no panic and, in contrast to earlier encounters in the mountains when the nervous trigger-happy tribesmen had given away their positions, the Bedouin on this occasion held their fire like seasoned troops. The few days of professional British training seemed to be paying off. Instead of the usual wild fusillades and frenzied stampedes, a deathly silence covered the town like a shroud. To make it even more eerie the approaches from the landward side were illumined by the stark white beams of searchlights from the five British warships lying off-shore, creating a death-trap out of the glacis of blazing light for any who ventured across it.

The Turks were quite unused to this kind of reception and lost their nerve in the awesome silence and the unrelenting blaze of light. Deceived into believing the place to be held by forces far beyond their strength, they stole away in the welcome darkness of the night and retreated into the hills between the steep banks of the Wadi Yenbo. As the first light of a new day broke upon the silent narrow streets and deserted little squares of the town, the bearded faces of its defenders broke into smiles as their weary bloodshot eyes strained into the distance and saw the approaches to be clear of enemy forces. Lawrence and Feisal were quickly among them, laughing and driving home the lesson that the night had brought them all. The Turks were no supermen; on the contrary, they could be made to run away without a shot fired against them. Arabia could be saved by scaring the wits out of the enemy.

These words, uttered at the time in derisory relief at their fortunate deliverance, were to prove more prophetic than anyone in the Arab or British forces could then have foreseen. The Turks' failure to press their attack against Yenbo was in fact the turning-point in the Hejaz war. The enemy had exhausted his pristine initiative. The long painful process of roll-back could now begin, provided that the Turks might always be prevented from engaging the Arab armies in pitched battle.

6

The Turkish reverse at the gates of Yenbo had now to be followed up. Lawrence went down to Rabegh to consult with Colonel Wilson about the next move. There he found Colonel Bremond who had come from Jidda to urge his plan for an Anglo-French assault on Medina. Bremond argued that the Arab Revolt had already shot its bolt and that it was now time for Britain and France to take over the conduct of operations, clear the Hejaz of Turkish forces and march on Damascus, unencumbered by the Arab armies. He made little attempt to conceal that, in accordance with the Sykes-Picot agreement, his instructions from Paris were to ensure that France should have unbridled control over Syria. Britain, he conceded, could have Mesopotamia for her reward and the Sherif of Mecca might be offered the kingdom of the Hejaz as compensation for his services.

"You do not seriously believe that these savages could run their own affairs after the pitiful display they have made against Medina," he mocked. "My dear friend, I know these people. I have commanded Arab troops in Morocco."

Lawrence retorted hotly that, if given the chance, the Arabs could and would prove the vigour of their movement. That was one very good reason why he wanted them to follow up the Turkish reverse at Yenbo and seize the initiative. It was, he added pointedly, why Bremond wanted British and French troops to usurp the function of the Sherif's armies and by landing in strength on the Arabian coast to make Hussein suspect in the eyes of his followers, who would then desert and leave him to the mercy of the Allies.

So the argument raged until Wilson arrived from Jidda and threw his weight behind his British compatriot. But Wilson brought one disturbing item of information that had just been telegraphed to him from Cairo. Murray had agreed after all to set aside an Anglo-French brigade to be held in reserve in Egypt for operations in the Hejaz and an advance party of officers under Colonel Newcombe was on its way to enquire into the problem of co-ordinating operations with the Arab armies. Realizing how this plan might play into Bremond's hands, Lawrence decided to act quickly to prevent these interferences with his own designs. Wilson's ideas for seizing the initiative coincided completely with his own thinking. The Turks were now in trouble. There was much sickness in their ranks and an attempt to capture Rabegh had just fizzled out in much the same way as their effort at Yenbo. They were being constantly harassed by Arab tribes, their food supplies were too low to maintain men in fighting trim and they were losing men and animals at an alarming rate. Fakhri Pasha was reported to be withdrawing to defensive positions around Medina.

This was then the moment to follow through and throw the enemy into confusion. Wilson's plan was for Zeid and Ali, whose nerve had been restored by the Yenbo success, to continue to hold the approaches to the Red Sea, while Abdulla undertook a flanking movement around Medina to threaten the Hejaz railway, the Turks' main artery of communication between Damascus and the Holy City. Feisal's rôle was to march on Wejh, another Red Sea port, one hundred and seventy miles north of Yenbo, and capture it with a force of ten thousand Juheina tribesmen. A squadron of six British warships under Captain Boyle would move northwards parallel to his advance, transporting five hundred regular Arab infantry and a few companies of British marines who would on the appointed day launch a converging attack from the sea. The day set for the synchronized assault was 28th January. The British ships would also keep the landborne forces supplied with food and fresh water, a task which could not otherwise have been performed along a desert track which provided few enough wells at the best of times and scarcely a single one that had not been poisoned by the Turks.

With the capture of Wejh, Lawrence and Wilson felt that the Turkish position in the Hejaz would become precarious in the extreme. The only port remaining to them on that coast would then be Akaba which was over five hundred miles north of Medina. Also with Wejh in Allied hands, added to Yenbo, Rabegh and Jidda, the supply problem for the Sherifian forces operating against Medina and the Hejaz railway would be greatly reduced. The only problem was that, in spite of the palpable advantages of this plan, Feisal stubbornly opposed it when Lawrence and Wilson returned to Yenbo to discuss the next phase of the campaign. Although he had recovered much of his confidence in the ability of his forces to defend themselves against Turkish assaults, the Emir was not at all happy with the idea of moving over to the offensive. Still less did the notion appeal to him of forsaking the security of Yenbo and Rabegh and striking out across nearly two hundred miles of waterless desert to capture a stronghold of unknown strength. Clearly the reverses which the Turks had inflicted upon him had not yet lost their effect.

Lawrence records that Feisal was finally overpersuaded by a guarantee of British naval support for Yenbo and Rabegh. At the same time the plan for Abdulla's flanking movement was changed so as to bring his five thousand irregulars to guard Feisal's line of retreat and to divert Turkish attention to the north of Medina and harass their caravans from the Persian Gulf. With these assurances Feisal agreed to the British plan and, on 14th January, after a brief visit to Abdulla to make sure of his co-operation, Lawrence took his place with the Emir at the head of his army. Lawrence describes the scene of primitive splendour as the expedition got under way.

Everyone burst out singing a full-throated song in honour of Emir Feisal and his family. The march became rather splendid and barbaric. First rode Feisal in white. Then Sharraf at his right in red head-cloth and henna-dyed tunic and cloak, myself on his left in white and scarlet, behind us three banners of faded crimson silk with gilt spikes, behind them the drummers playing a march, and behind them again the wild mass of twelve hundred bouncing camels of the bodyguard, packed as closely as they could move, the men in every variety of coloured clothes and the camels nearly as brilliant in their trappings. We filled the valley to its banks with our flashing stream.

For the first half of the distance the march remained the same triumphal procession. The high spirits of the Arabs received an extra tonic when they learned after a few days that Abdulla had captured a Turkish caravan with twenty thousand pounds of gold and that Ali's and Zeid's patrols had penetrated to the gates of Medina. Better still in the way of news for the Juheina tribesmen came a report from Abdulla that the guardian of the captured gold who had been made prisoner was a notorious Turkish adventurer, Eshref Bey. Born a brigand, Eshref had later become a revolutionary and was exiled by the Turkish Sultan for five years. Escaping one day from his gaol he kidnapped the governor's son and vanished into the hills where he held the boy to ransom. To get his son back the governor had been forced to pay five hundred pounds and to grant Eshref liberty on parole. This he had used to prey upon the desert caravans, making little distinction between between those of the Turks and those of the local tribesmen and exacting tribute from their drivers at some appropriate place such as a river bridge or a precipitous mountain pass. Those who could not or would not pay he simply threw into the river or down the ravine. After the advent of the Young Turks he had been taken on as a hired assassin for Enver Pasha and was about to retire on his savings from this lucrative employment when war broke out and his services were again in demand for various subversive missions. When he was taken by Abdulla, he was on his way to open up communications with the isolated Turkish garrisons in the Yemen and to distribute gold to the tribes to buy them off joining the Arab revolt.

The news of Eshref's capture came as a double dose of good news to Feisal's men. It offered recompense for the money which this outlaw had exacted from them and it showed that Abdulla was actively pressing the Turks in his sector. The tide of ill-fortune seemed to have turned and in the glad faces about the camp that night, as Abdulla's messengers told and retold their story, glowed the hope that victory was already at hand. Lawrence joined in the noisy rejoicing. His plans were working out well. The Turks were being pushed onto the defensive.

7

Probably the only jarring note in Feisal's army at this stage of the march was the unhappy relationship between Lawrence and Lieutenant Vickery, a fanatical young British officer serving under Colonel Newcombe who had been attached to the Wejh expedition. Lawrence found no difficulty in working with Newcombe, whom he knew well from Cairo and their joint exploration of Sinai. Newcombe had humour and in their hopes and designs for the Arab movement they were at one. But Vickery was altogether different, aloof and always keeping his distance in his relations with the Arabs. A professional soldier utterly dedicated to the military calling, he did not conceal his opinion that Lawrence was militarily incompetent and that his political approach to the Arab movement was absurd. The importance of the march of Feisal's army as a propaganda demonstration and a recruiting drive was completely lost on his blinkered senses—although from every village and desert camp which they passed on their journey new adherents came forth in their hundreds to swell the ranks.

Another cause of friction was Vickery's fluent knowledge of Arabic and the experience of desert warfare which he had come by as a British officer commanding native troops in the Sudan. Jealous of his position with Feisal and the Arab army, Lawrence regarded Vickery as a potential rival and at the outset of the march sought every opportunity to humiliate and undermine him in the eyes of Feisal's troops. During this early part of the Arab revolt Lawrence alternated between bouts of great self-confidence and over-sensitivity about his status. Though Cairo had confirmed him as liaison officer with Feisal he was in military matters subject to the orders of Colonel Joyce, the senior British officer with the Sherif's armies, and in political affairs was answerable to the Arab Bureau, who dealt with Hussein through Colonel Wilson. Not until General Allenby took over as Commander-in-Chief and decided to deal with Lawrence directly and to short-circuit the chain of command did he become his own master.

The knowledge that Vickery had infinitely more experience of fighting in these conditions as well as a better grasp of Arabic—Lawrence, contrary to popular belief, spoke the language with an atrocious accent—was enough to implant a fear of Vickery taking over his job. Like a jealous mistress threatened by the charms of some rival courtesan, Lawrence set upon his British colleague and found every way to make life impossible for him. So much bitter mutual resentment could only end one way, and, at the halfway stage on the journey to Wejh, Vickery left to join Boyle's naval expedition thankful for this avenue of escape from the barbed tongue of his tormentor.

Hardly had Vickery left than Feisal's expedition ran into trouble. Exhausted by the speed of the initial advance—over a hundred miles in a week—they could not keep up the pace. They were now in unknown and also largely uninhabited territory, which provided neither food, water nor information—an unwelcome contrast to their triumphal procession through the villages and settlements on the first part of the journey. Their next rendezvous with Boyle's ships at Habban, fifty miles short of Wejh, was two days' march away and they were already two days behind schedule.

Newcombe undertook to ride on ahead and catch up with Boyle. If he could not persuade the navy to postpone the attack and wait for Feisal, he would at least insist on one ship being sent back after she had discharged her landing party to meet the partisans at Habban, about twenty miles from Wejh, and replenish their supplies of food and water. Meanwhile Feisal's forces dragged their weary way across the desolate featureless desert whipped by a cold north wind. Morale had sunk very low and discipline, which among proud tribesmen unused to being given orders could never be according to western standards, was fast disappearing altogether. Seizing every opportunity to relieve the painful tedium of the march, the Bedouin would gallop off in pursuit of any stray herd of camels, never pausing to think whose they might be. After one such adventure, Feisal was forced personally to discipline the offenders with his camel-stick when he discovered that the booty belonged to the Billi tribe to whom he had only recently sent letters assuring them of his warmest friendship and seeking their co-operation for his further advances through their territory beyond Wejh.

The same night they reached Habban an exhausted rabble, stumbling down the beach to the ship's boats that waited offshore with water for them and their animals. As they drank slowly, to savour fully the fresh clear water, the thunder of distant guns rolled in on the keen north wind. Feisal and Lawrence exchanged glances, each sadly admitting to the other that Boyle had decided not to wait for them before launching his attack upon Wejh. On board the *Hardinge,* which had been sent back to provision Feisal's troops, they learned that Boyle had decided to strike for fear that any delay would have allowed the Turks either to escape or to reinforce their positions. It seemed from the rumble of gunfire that the battle was not yet over; but it could not last much longer as the enemy garrison was reported to number only a third of the Anglo-Arab landing party and to have no guns to match the fire-power of the British warships.

Feisal looked a disappointed man as he returned to the shore to rally his men for the last stretch of the long trek to Wejh. The brave hopes and slogans with which he and his followers had sung their way out of Yenbo lay bruised and thwarted in the dust of a desert camp fifty miles on the wrong side of their objective. For Lawrence, too, this initial forestalling of his plan for the first successful Arab offensive was a sad disappointment, made more galling still by the reflection that the egregious Vickery must have led the Arab infantry in the assault on the town.

Three days later when the Arab army arrived in Wejh—now firmly held by the Anglo-Arab force— Lawrence's surmise was confirmed by Vickery in person. Determined not to spare his former tormentor any humiliation, Vickery's eyes danced with a gleam of fanaticism as he told in detail of the fighting that had taken place before the town fell. A model military operation, he concluded, with only twenty killed. Lawrence could stand no more. Bitterly lashing out at Vickery he retorted that he could not accept the professional soldier's view that twenty lives were twenty chattels to be traded for a military success. The Arab infantrymen who had been killed were friends who trusted in British leadership. Had the attack been delayed until Feisal's army arrived, they need not have died. The Turks would have surrendered without a fight, seeing how vastly outnumbered they were. This had been an unnecessary action with unnecessary casualties and was not only a waste but a sin.

After this outburst, Lawrence made a tour of the town. What he saw did little to relieve his feelings. The Arab landing party had sacked the place and carried off everything of value that they could find. Shops had been broken open, houses ransacked, cupboards and chests smashed, even mattresses had been bayoneted in the frantic search for hidden treasure; and what the troops had not laid waste had been pulverized by the navy's guns, mud walls offering no resistance to the pounding of high explosive shells.

Sickened by such widespread devastation, Lawrence returned to his tent to brood on the situation of the revolt. On balance the position was encouraging. They had learned much from the march from Yenbo, although its ending was a deep disappointment. The Arab movement had been firmly established throughout the Hejaz, where it was now virtually unopposed except in Medina, and that city could be safely bypassed for the time being. Altogether it seemed he had a good account of his stewardship in Arabia to give to G.H.Q.: upon which self-satisfying thought he began to reflect that, judged against the gains they had made, Vickery's impatience might have been justified after all and that his own outburst had perhaps been unreasonably harsh.

8

When the news of the capture of Wejh reached Colonel Bremond in Jidda he was furious. Nobody had told him of this operation and he felt bitterly slighted by his British allies. His ill-temper was not improved when simultaneously with this unwelcome shock he received a severe reprimand from home. General Joffre, French Commander-in-Chief, had telegraphed from Paris to say that Bremond's attitude was giving the British and the Arabs the dangerous impression that France had designs on Syria and was deliberately trying to confine the Arabs to the Hejaz. "This state of mind," Joffre commented ambiguously, "could have serious consequences on the development of our plans in the Levant."

Bremond guessed that this reproof for having let the cat out of the bag was the result of Lawrence complaining to Cairo about his attitude. Anglo-French military co-operation in the Near East theatre of operations had never been a very happy affair. At G.H.Q. the French were held in only slightly less contempt than the Arabs. The cynical suggestion that France would fight to the last Englishman was a standing joke in British army circles, where carping remarks would frequently be exchanged about the antiquity of French equipment—the Arabs threw away the rifles which the French gave them as useless—and the ragged appearance of the Algerian troops which were France's principal contribution to the Allied armies—even the French officers commanding these units were never properly turned out. There was no hesitation therefore at G.H.Q. when Lawrence complained of Bremond's anti-British and anti-Arab manoeuvres in Jidda, in passing his reports on to London and in requesting that immediate remonstrances be made to the French Government.

But Bremond was not a man to give up because he had been slighted by his allies and reprimanded by his superiors in the space of a few hours. A successful intriguer requires a cool temper. So, swallowing his rage, he made for Cairo to try once more to get his plans adopted for the future conduct of operations in Arabia. There he found Lawrence flushed with delight at discovering that the success of the Arab advance had won him admiration and support in the most unexpected quarters. Bremond greeted his British colleague warmly, offering him his heartfelt congratulations on his important achievement in capturing Wejh.

"I was one of those who always believed that you had considerable military talents," he said, his tongue almost piercing his cheek. "Now you have proved it and I am encouraged to ask you to help me in my plans for extending your successes." With that Bremond proceeded to outline his plans for an Anglo-French assault on Akaba, the only port on the Red Sea coast still in Turkish hands. This, he said, would open up a supply line for the Allied forces, including the main body coming up from Suez, to push on northwards to the Jordan Valley and then into Syria. What Bremond did not say was that his proposed attack on Akaba was designed as much to head off the Arabs and confine them to the Hejaz as to open a supply port for operations northwards. But Lawrence had guessed this from the start of the Frenchman's exposition; and Lawrence had his own plans for taking Akaba with Feisal's Arab army, plans which he had just finished expounding to a conference at G.H.Q. When Bremond announced that he intended to go and put his proposals to Feisal, Lawrence therefore decided to forestall him and to forewarn his King-elect of these French designs upon his kingdom.

Scurrying off to Wejh, Lawrence told Feisal of the Frenchman's intentions, so that when Bremond arrived ten days later the Emir was well prepared and handled himself with consummate skill. When Bremond, as a sweetener, presented him with half-a-dozen Hotchkiss machine-guns, Feisal thanked him but asked for the use of the battery of mountain guns which the French had been keeping in idleness at Suez. Without this type of equipment, he said, he could not match the Turks in fire-power, for they had French artillery! Stung by this barb, Bremond retorted that guns were useless to the Arabs, who should "climb about the country like goats and tear up the railway." Now it was Feisal's turn to be angry, for the metaphor could scarcely have been ruder in the Arabic tongue. Had his French visitor ever tried to climb like a goat, he asked, surveying the colonel's tall ungainly proportions? Bremond ignored the question and decided to come to the point. He stressed the importance to the Arabs of getting the Turks out of Akaba and suggested that Feisal should press for an Allied landing to capture the port. Feisal's eyes wore an artless expression, as he replied that he really could not ask for this so soon after the help he had received from the British in the capture of Wejh.

In the end Bremond had to give up and content himself with a parting shot at Lawrence, whose spitefully smiling countenance as he rose to take his leave irritated him almost beyond endurance. Looking at Lawrence, he remarked to Feisal that he should demand that the British armoured cars at Suez be sent to Wejh. Lawrence in a flash replied that they were already on their way. A deep red flush spread across the luckless Bremond's cheeks as he opened his mouth to speak, then thought better of it and strode arrogantly out into the night.

Bremond had shot his bolt. As Lawrence discovered when he left for Cairo a few days later, the

Frenchman had made no impression on G.H.Q. with his Akaba plan. Thereafter this somewhat tragic intriguer returned to Jidda where his efforts were confined to making mischief—not always without success—between Abdulla and the British. These further intrigues resulted in the British Ambassador in Paris demanding in May 1917, on instructions from the Foreign Office, that the crafty colonel be recalled immediately from the Hejaz. The demand was not met; but Bremond was thereafter left without support from his government. By that time the attentions of his employers in Paris had in any case switched from the Hejaz, which had become a backwater, to Syria, which beckoned with the promise of new territorial gains for France's empire overseas.

❖   ❖   ❖

For more than two months following the capture of Wejh Feisal's army was kept busy organizing and equipping itself for the next move. Money and stores were now pouring in from Egypt. Guns, machine-guns, rifles, ammunition—even a radio station—were landed from the British transports that called in a steady stream to empty their well-packed holds into the eager arms of Britain's new-found allies.

New recruits arrived to swell the ranks. Jaafar Pasha was among them. Born a Baghdadi, this Falstaffian figure had been trained for military service in the German army and had risen to the rank of colonel in the Turkish service. He commanded the Turkish cavalry in the campaign against the British in Cyrenaica and, after several battles in which he showed astonishing physical courage, was taken prisoner. He had all but escaped from captivity—all but his weight, that is, for when he had let himself down from his prison window on a rope of sheets the rope broke under the strain and he fell with a resounding splash into the prison moat, thereby alerting every sentry for miles around. When he heard of the Arab revolt and of the execution of his Syrian friends in Damascus, Jaafar realized that he had all along been on the wrong side and offered his services at once to the Allies. Feisal, who remembered his reputation for bravery and acknowledged his gifts of leadership, wanted Jaafar as his Commander-in-Chief, but Sherif Hussein allowed his prejudices against Mesopotamians to influence his judgement and refused to employ Jaafar. Feisal eventually accepted this corpulent and courageous rebel into his army on his own responsibility.

Other fighting men arrived to pledge themselves to Feisal's service, including Nawwaf, eldest son of Nuri Shaalan who had helped the Emir to escape from Damascus. The combination of a little success, hatred of the Turks and the lure of arms now arriving in plentiful quantities from Cairo was proving a powerful magnet to the tribal leaders from the north. Then, one day in April, Feisal's guest-master hurried into his tent in the middle of a conference with Lawrence and whispered excitedly in the Emir's ear. Feisal's eyes brightened and, with a vain effort to appear calm, he said breathlessly, "Auda is here." A second later the tent-flap was drawn back and there appeared a tall, strong figure with a gaunt, dramatic face.

This was Auda abu Tayi, the paramount Sheikh of the Howeitat tribe and one of the most legendary desert chiefs of this or any other time, a man who personally embodied the Bedouin tradition of combining brigandage with a nomadic pastoral existence, whose pillaging and raiding had become a desert legend. Auda had spent the past four decades in fights and forays against other nomadic tribes of northern Arabia, the settled peoples of the Syrian border regions and, above all, the hated Turks. Law—or outlaw—unto himself, he had personally killed seventy-five Arabs and had lost count of the score of Turks, he had been wounded thirteen times and married twenty-eight. Though prone to fits of anger that made him a wild beast to be assuaged only by a killing, he could also be cool and calculating when the need arose. Lawrence says of him, "He saw life as a saga. All the events in it were significant; all personages in contact with him heroic." And none was more heroic in his own eyes than himself, of whom he always spoke in the third person. A lover of stories of battles and raids, he always cast himself in the principal rôle and in the absence of an audience would sometimes sing or recite to himself songs or poems extolling his own victories. Yet withal he could be "modest, as simple as a child, direct, honest, kindhearted and warmly loved even by those to whom he was most embarrassing—his friends."

It was a remarkable meeting of two men, utterly different in character and temperament, yet destined to work as partners from now on in the common cause that was to take them together to Damascus. And, as they stood for a moment silently smiling at one another, the prophet and the warrior, Lawrence knew that they had found the combination of power and precept that would carry the Arab armies to victory.

Auda's arrival to join Feisal could not have been more timely. Feisal knew that, without a guarantee of safe conduct from the Howeitat who inhabited the area between Wejh and Maan, any advance northwards would be hazardous in the extreme. To expose his army to the maraudings of Auda's men across three hundred miles of desert would have been sheer lunacy. But now here was the great robber baron personally pledging himself to the Sherifian service, saluting Feisal as "Our Lord, the Commander of the Faithful" and even complaining of the long delay of his army's advance from Yenbo.

Besides assuring Feisal of an uninterrupted passage through the Howeitat's domains, Auda's adherence served another critically important purpose. Once the news had spread, other tribes, who had been sitting on the fence uncertain of whether to join actively in the Arab revolt, hastened to Feisal's side. One of the most difficult tasks which had confronted the Emir from the outset of his movement had been to overcome the traditional feuds and vendettas which had divided the tribes of Arabia from time immemorial.

Judged by logical standards, it seems inexcusable and nonsensical that the Arabs, with so much to gain from overthrowing their Turkish masters, should not have been ready and anxious to compose their differences and join together to destroy their oppressors, once the banner of revolt had been raised in Mecca and help was forthcoming from Britain. But the Arab has never been one to govern his temper or determine his attitude by the use of logic. Those who had been trained as soldiers of the Turkish army, although unaffected by tribal hatreds, were, like Feisal and his court, suspicious of their self-appointed liberators. More educated and sophisticated than their desert brethren, they believed that the promises of British and French help were but a cover for a deep-laid plan to seize Arabia on the pretext of delivering it. Those who had not been educated to these levels of suspicion feared to cast their lot with the Sherifian army lest some neighbouring tribe with whom a blood feud existed, dating perhaps from a murder committed several decades ago, might take advantage from the absence of their best warriors and camels to wreak their vengeance. Or, more simply, they disliked the idea of fighting on the same side as those whom they had been brought up to regard as traditional tribal enemies.

Probably the greatest achievement of Feisal and Lawrence between 1916 and 1918 was their success in gaining the trust and allegiance of these varied groups of Arab opinion and in welding such incompatible elements as the tribes of Arabia into a fighting unit alongside the Allies. Some critics may sneer and say that it was all done with gold; but bribery, as Lawrence found for himself, is a double-edged sword and can as easily make enemies of those who feel they have had too little as it may make associates of those who have had enough. That gold played some part is beyond question; but patience, understanding and example were probably in the long run far more important assistants and in these three qualities none were richer than the triumvirate of Feisal, Lawrence and Auda.

9

Besides its political and military significance, the addition of Auda and his Howeitat clan to the cause gave a much needed uplift to Lawrence's morale. He had just returned from a visit to the Emir Abdulla at Abu Markha. Dogged by misfortune and sickness, this journey of one hundred and twenty-five miles into the coastal mountains south-east of Wejh could hardly have been more depressing. For a fit man this six-day camel ride would have been a severe enough test. But Lawrence was ill with fever and dysentery when he set out and was only kept going by his extraordinary determination never to give way to physical suffering, an endurance so great at times as to suggest that he gained a spiritual exhilaration from pain. The going was appallingly rough and the route lay through an endless succession of sinister ravines and along zigzagging mountain paths so narrow and steep that the camels had to be dragged along dismounted in order to make any progress at all. In the black lava valleys the men were subjected to a suffocating heat and the camels winced with pain at every step among the sharp hot cinders. In the mountains men and beasts shivered in a freezing rain.

Lawrence's party had not been long on its way when disputes began between the Bedouin and the Ageylis, men of a settled tribe from the Nejd in the heart of the Arabian peninsula. One evening at the end of a long and painful march Lawrence was resting and waiting for his escort to prepare a meal when

he heard a shot. One of the Ageylis had been murdered by an Algerian Moor and lay with a bullet
through his brain. Lawrence knew he must act
quickly. The Ageylis would demand blood for blood
and this could lead to counter demands by the fellows
of the Moor, until his entire escort might be exter-
minated by the satisfaction of the blood feud's rites.
Staging a summary trial of the murderer, who made
no attempt to deny his crime, Lawrence resisted the
demands of the Ageylis to be allowed to execute the
Moor themselves and, marching his prisoner into a
narrow gully, shot him with his revolver.

Three days later Lawrence reached Abu Markha
and collapsed into delirium, his fevered brain floun-
dering in a world of nightmares in which he wandered naked across endless stretches of black lava
pursued by the dead Moor. For several days he lay
demented like this before the fever abated enough to
allow his mind to function while he continued to rest
his exhausted body.

Lying back in one of Abdulla's tents Lawrence
went over and over again the lessons which he and
Feisal had so far learned from the Hejaz campaign.
First and foremost he now knew that the best way to
defeat the Turks was to avoid them. The Arab army
was no good in a pitched battle with trained troops,
whether in attack or defence. Though fearless and
ferocious in hot blood, they had little stomach for
carrying on the fight if the first assault should be repulsed and would prefer to put off returning to the
charge until some other day. Every time the Turks
had attacked the Arabs, or vice versa, the Arabs had
lost heavily, had indeed all but lost the Hejaz. But,
whenever the Arabs had circumvented the enemy and
fallen upon some lightly held town or village, they
had won. Thus the second lesson to be applied to the
future was to use the Arabs' natural advantages of
speed and surprise to harass the Turks constantly
and keep them bottled up in Medina, while the

Arabs made a dash for Damascus and the Allies pushed on through Sinai and Palestine.

Applying these principles to the immediate future, the next move clearly had to be the capture of Akaba by Feisal's forces. Abdulla's part in this operation would be to attack the Hejaz railway and keep it cut, so as to prevent Fakhri's men escaping or coming to the rescue of the Akaba garrison. But when Lawrence put the plan to the Emir he was apathetic and bored by the Arab war. In the past few months Abdulla had become self-indulgent and shallow. All he wanted to talk about was the war in France or the crowned heads of Europe. Lawrence knew that he had been got at by Bremond who, having failed to talk Feisal out of capturing Damascus, had been concentrating his wiles on Abdulla and surrounding him with French advisers. Abdulla had in fact confronted Lawrence with a letter from Bremond purporting to warn him that the British were "wrapping up the Arabs" and using them for their own ulterior designs in the Hejaz, in Egypt and Mesopotamia. When the Emir asked for an explanation, Lawrence cunningly replied that he hoped Abdulla would begin to distrust the British when they started intriguing against their allies.

The Emir's second-in-command, Sherif Shakir, was a very different type to his master. A tall, fair twenty-nine-year-old, the son of a Circassian mother, Shakir had been in Sherif Hussein's service more as a diplomatic envoy to the Khedive of Egypt than as a soldier. But his big restless eyes beamed above his pock-marked cheeks as he agreed there and then to join Lawrence in a trial raid on the Hejaz railway. Though still weak from the effects of dysentery and fever, Lawrence knew he must go through with the exercise, if only not to dissipate the zeal of Shakir and those around Abdulla who favoured more action.

So he set off with Shakir, a score of Juheina and Ateiba tribesmen, a camel train of high explosives and, as guide for the expedition, an elderly Bedouin called Dakhil-Allah, who was the hereditary Lawman of the Juheina and whose last job as a desert scout had been to guide the abortive Turkish expedition to Yenbo! Their plan was to destroy a railway station and round up its garrison; but, since only a third of the number of Arab irregulars that Shakir had arranged turned up, they had to be content with sabotaging a few miles of track and a couple of locomotives. Nevertheless Lawrence gained some valuable experience in the use of high explosive mines—weapons with which he and his Arabs were destined to kill far more Turks and inflict far more damage on the enemy than with the more conventional artillery of assault. Also he proved to himself that the Hejaz railway could without difficulty be kept constantly cut. Finally he gained another piece of intelligence about himself that was of great value. He had shown that by a supreme effort of willpower he could carry on fighting and marching beyond the limits even of extraordinary endurance. He was able to overcome the natural frailties of his slight unmuscular frame and could go farther and faster than the toughest of the hardened warriors he had to lead.

10

Feisal gave a banquet to celebrate Auda's arrival, which was attended, apart from Lawrence, by the Emir's young cousin and second-in-command, Sherif Nasir of Medina, and other sheikhly relatives of the host and his guest of honour. As the meal was about to begin, Auda leapt to his feet and rushed from the tent. Lawrence followed only to find the ferocious old Bedouin beating his false teeth to powder with a stone. "I had forgotten," Auda explained, "Jemal Pasha gave me these. I was eating my lord's bread with Turkish teeth!" A splendid gesture, considering that these were his only dentures and he had to wait three months before he could get them replaced with a British set sent from Egypt—and Auda was a prodigious eater!

After the meal a council of war followed, at which virtually the entire Arab army seemed to be present. In accordance with custom every man was entitled to speak his mind at such conferences and suggest to his leader what he felt should be the plan of action, in the same way as he had the right under tribal law to be heard by the tribal sheikh, if he had a grievance or dispute to air. Having heard all the arguments and counter-arguments the Commander would then decide for himself what the plans and orders should be. The orders would then be given out in great detail, since once his blood is up the Arab simply will not hear any orders given in the heat of battle.

It was a most important conference for Lawrence, for it was essential to him that the Arabs should ac-

cept his plan for taking Akaba as the next move.
Clayton had been sending him urgent messages saying that the General Staff had reason to believe
that Fakhri Pasha had been ordered to evacuate
Medina. Cairo wanted the Arab armies to make every
effort to capture Medina and destroy its garrison as
they left. Sir Archibald Murray's attack on Gaza had
just started and this Arab operation would be its
counterpart. Colonel Joyce and Newcombe both believed Medina could be taken by seizing and holding a stretch of the Hejaz railway and so starving the
Turks into surrendering or making a bolt for it.
But Lawrence was convinced from his ruminations at
Abu Markha that the Arabs should not risk a frontal
assault against a well-trained and well-equipped Turkish force. The only gain would be in the ammunition
expended by the enemy. Besides Fakhri should be encouraged to keep his garrison of 15,000 men in
Medina where they could do no harm. This could be
contrived by constant harassing attacks on the railway which would prevent sufficient reinforcements
getting through to enable the Turks to take the offensive and break out towards the sea. Most important of all, the road to Damascus lay through
Akaba to the north and Medina was in the opposite direction.

Lawrence had not, however, succeeded in persuading his superiors to his way of thinking and had
therefore decided that, while the bulk of Feisal's
forces might have to follow Joyce's lead and concentrate on the railway, he personally would go
his own way, if he could get a small band of Arabs
to go with him. Having politely but firmly informed
Clayton to this effect, he had put his ideas to Feisal.
The Emir had not been too keen on an Akaba expedition until Auda joined up, but was now in full
agreement.

After some preliminary debate, Lawrence outlined his plan of action to the assembly. The
route to Akaba was too long and tough a journey

to permit them to take any heavy equipment such as guns or machine-guns or bulky stores of food. Accordingly he proposed to take a small detachment of irregulars and march in an encircling movement to the Howeitat country two hundred miles to the northeast. There he would raise a mobile camel force from the local Howeitat clans and with this force would rush Akaba from the east. This, according to intelligence reports, was the unguarded side, since the town's defences all faced west towards the sea.

To Lawrence's relief Auda could hardly wait to endorse this plan. Brushing aside all argument, he said that anything could be done with enough dynamite and money. Also he could pledge his word that the Howeitat would help supply all that was necessary for the attack. Feisal agreed too and, after some further discussion about the composition of the force and the route of the march, the decision was taken and the council of war dismissed.

On 9th May Lawrence, Auda and his cousin Mohammed el Dheilan, Sherif Nasir and a Damascene Sheikh called Nesib el-Bekri left Wejh, accompanied by thirty-five Ageyli camel men, armed only with rifles and carrying forty-five pounds of flour per man and half-a-dozen black goat-skin tents. The only item of abundance in the expedition's frugal equipment was the twenty thousand pounds in gold which Feisal gave Lawrence from his British fund to help him raise the supplies he would need on the journey and for the final assault. Feisal himself stayed behind to take part, under Joyce's direction, in the British planned offensive against the Hejaz railway.

They made a strange combination—Auda, the brigand chief with his incomparable knowledge of the desert; Nasir, the rich and cultivated aristocrat who would have looked more at home in his well-kept garden-palace than on the back of a camel riding across a wilderness; Nesib, a musical and poetic creature whom the Turks had sentenced to death for his complicity in Feisal's escape; and Lawrence, the personal adventurer who had cast his lot with the Arab peoples, never exactly certain how much he was serving their cause and how much he was bending them to serve his; a man caught up in a dream of empire with his chosen prophet as the emperor and himself the power behind the throne, the diminutive captain and commoner constantly trying on a prince's crown.

It was at this stage of his odyssey that Lawrence began to identify himself increasingly with his Arab comrades-in-arms. Prior to his departure from Wejh, he had been the still obedient, though always argumentative, subordinate of Colonel Joyce and his military and political bosses in Cairo. But, in writing as he did to Clayton and in galloping off to Akaba on his own with only a small intimate band of Arabs for fellowship, he severed or at least drastically loosened this link with his superiors and became from now on more a representative of Feisal to the British High Command than a liaison officer of G.H.Q. with the Arab army.

The extent to which Lawrence had become an Arab was evident not only in his dress—Bedouin robe, head-dress and sandals—and in his ready acceptance of the spartan and unsavoury living conditions of these long marches, but also in his entire mental approach. He had become a creature of the desert, a guerilla fighter, an Arab chieftain. By day he would delight in driving himself and leading his warriors farther and faster than even the best of them were wont to go, blowing up railways, rounding up Turks and marching, always marching, towards Damascus. By night, huddled for warmth against his Bedouin comrades in some mountain bivouac around the long-spouted coffee pot, he liked nothing better than to hear the Ageylis tell the stories of love, war, travel or magic for which their tribe was famous and to laugh uproariously at some Rabelaisian love-tale or listen apparently spellbound to some story of magic.

A few days out from Wejh, Lawrence was resting after a hard day's march when two young Ageylis ran to him and pleaded for his mercy. Never having seen them before, he asked who they were and why they were so agitated. The elder of the two boys, a strong virile youth, announced breathlessly that his name was Daud and his friend, who had a soft and rather beautiful face, almost girlish, with innocent eyes, was Farraj. For a prank Farraj had tried to set fire to one of the Ageyli tents and the occupant, an Ageyli captain named Saad, was going to beat him if Lawrence did not intercede on his behalf. Upon enquiry, Saad adamantly insisted that an example must be made of the culprit, but agreed to allow his friend Daud to share the punishment; whereupon Daud kissed Lawrence's hand and Saad's and went off rejoicing. The next day the two boys were back entreating Lawrence to take them into his service. Attracted by their impish humour and their curious mutual friendship—an example, as Lawrence put it, "of the eastern boy and boy affection which the segregation of women made inevitable"—he accepted them and so formed the nucleus of that inter-tribal collection of ruffians that was to be his bodyguard from Akaba onwards.

Day after day the long trek continued, first over craggy mountain passes, then across seemingly interminable stretches of black lava desert, then mile upon arid mile of sand and scrub, guided only by the uncanny instinct and experience of Auda. Lawrence says of this journey, "Nothing in the march was normal or reassuring. We felt we were in an ominous land, incapable of life, hostile even to the passing of life, except painfully along such sparse roads as time had laid across its face. We were forced into a single file of weary camels, picking a hesitant way step by step through the boulders for hour after hour." And so it must have seemed as the expedition plodded its thirsty way across what in summer is one of the hottest and dryest places on earth, where no sign of life was to be seen, no tracks of gazelle, no birds, not even a rat or a lizard, and where across the hollow spaces of the pitiless plain the Khamsin wind with its blast of furnace heat lashed their faces with tiny shrapnel particles of sand.

One hundred and fifty miles and ten days' march from Wejh they crossed the Hejaz railway, pausing to blow up a stretch of the track and pull down a few telegraph poles. Then on across the two-hundred-mile stretch of the waterless Nefudh desert to the wells of Arfaja, on the edge of the Wadi Sirhan, Auda's home ground and the property of his Howeitat tribesmen. This section of the trek took another eight days, during which Lawrence was to prove once more his self-absorption in the Bedouin way of life. On a particularly weary and waterless stretch of the march he noticed that one of his party was missing. A quick look round showed a camel shuffling along in the rear of the caravan complete with saddle-bags, rifle and food, but no rider. The camel was identified as belonging to the most unpopular and worthless member of the expedition, one Gasim, a bad-tempered shirker who had grumbled his way from Wejh, aggravating everybody by his shiftless unco-operative attitude. Rather than trade on his status as a foreigner by sending one of the Ageylis back to find the straggler and although even the sheikhs—Auda, Nasir and Nesib—thought that in this case the progress of the expedition should not be imperilled for one man, Lawrence went back and found Gasim almost crazy with thirst and moaning with the fear of approaching death. When they rejoined the others, Auda looked contemptuously at the wretched Gasim and spat the words, "For that thing, not worth a camel's price." Lawrence laughed. "Not worth a half-crown, Auda," he replied. Auda laughed too and for the rest of the day's trek rode alongside Gasim, making him repeat the price they had agreed for him and repeating Lawrence's little joke as his own to every camel man in the party.

On 27th May, eighteen days after setting out from Wejh, the expedition reached Arfaja. A sorry sight they presented as with their mangy, starving camels they stumbled into the oasis to drink the brackish water of its wells that tasted delicious to their parched throats. Hardly had they slaked their thirst, however, when the alarm was sounded and they found themselves attacked by a group of Bedouin marauders from the Shammar tribe, long-time enemies of the Howeitat. The attack was beaten off, largely thanks to a courageous camel charge led by Mohammed, Auda's cousin. But Auda decided to push on and seek the security of the main body of Howeitat on the edge of the Wadi Sirhan.

Auda also had other business to transact—a non-aggression pact with the old desert fox Nuri Shaalan, Sheikh of the Sirhan, Emir of the Ruwalla tribe and fourth among the princes of Arabia. Though Nuri had helped Feisal to escape from Damascus he had not yet declared himself openly for the Arab Revolt. Since his tribal area marched with the Howeitat in the Wadi Sirhan, it was essential to buy or talk Nuri into pursuing a policy of inaction, while Auda and Lawrence were recruiting and organizing the Howeitat tribesmen for the attack on Akaba, and to persuade him to leave their villages unmolested while the menfolk were away. Auda was also to put to him Feisal's idea that Nuri should nominally declare his adherence to Turkey. This would satisfy Jemal Pasha that he had no need to send troops to patrol this area, and so leave Auda and Lawrence free to prepare their futher expedition.

Such deception was very necessary, for the whole Sirhan area was soon in a ferment of excitement with tribesmen pouring down in hundreds to join the Arab revolt, when the news got abroad of Auda's coming and of its purpose. There was much wild talk—which might all too soon reach Turkish ears

—of raising an army to take Damascus there and then. Nor was this kind of talk confined to the wild men. A plan for an immediate invasion of Syria was seriously suggested to Lawrence by Nesib el Bekri, the Damascene Sheikh. The Turks would be taken by surprise, he argued, and the response to Auda's call for recruits showed that the whole country would rise as one man to welcome their liberators. Besides, they were now no further from Damascus than they were from Akaba. Why then go in the opposite direction to their objective when it lay within their grasp?

But Lawrence was not that much of a gambler. He might have staked his future on capturing Akaba against the orders of his superiors because Akaba was necessary to extend the Arab front and to link up with the British in Sinai; but Damascus at this stage, no. It would be madness, he argued with Nesib, so to expose the Arab movement with "Feisal yet in Wejh, the British yet the wrong side of Gaza, the new Turkish army massing in Aleppo. . . ." Still Nesib's hot-headed thinking made its appeal to Auda and Nasir and it took all Lawrence's powers of artifice to head them off this dangerous digression.

11

Although Lawrence had rejected Nesib's plan for an immediate surge forward into Syria as wildly over-ambitious, the argument had planted in his mind the germ of another idea only slightly less fraught with danger for him personally. This was to make a quick trip to Damascus to see for himself how things were in the city of his dreams. Just exactly what he sought and what he expected to find is still a mystery. Lawrence was always very reticent about it, saying merely that he went "to see the more important of Feisal's secret friends and to study key-positions of our future campaign." But he admits that "the results were incommensurate with the risks. . . ." Indeed it is difficult to see what this hazardous exploit could have accomplished that could not have been achieved by messages relayed by one or several of the secret agents who plied continuously between Damascus and the Arab armies, unless Lawrence was planning an early offensive in Syria. We are therefore left with the conclusion that it was as likely as not one of those compulsive acts of bravado by which he sought constantly to prove himself to himself and to his Arab comrades.

Back in camp among the Howeitat preparations for the march on Akaba were going ahead. Auda had returned well satisfied with his encounter with Nuri Shaalan and divided his time between proselytizing among his tribes, recruiting men and material for the march and partaking of huge banquets of greasy rice and mutton proffered by the hospitable Howeitat sheikhs to their ever-hungry lord.

Lawrence returned from Syria on 16th June and three days later the expedition moved off to Akaba. A very different force from the little band that had struggled up from Wejh, Auda's men now numbered more than five hundred, each one mounted on a fast camel and eager for the foray and still more for the loot that he expected would be his when Akaba had been taken. Some of them did not have to wait that long to stuff their saddle-bags with Turkish loot. Lawrence, accompanied by Auda's nephew, Zaal, and a hundred men, led a diversionary attack northwards against the Hejaz railway between Amman and Deraa to lead the Turks off the scent of the Akaba trail. This involved a forced march of a hundred miles, which they covered in thirty-six hours, riding day and night in six-hour spells with intervals of one or two hours for rest. After blowing up a stretch of the track—they had hoped for a train but were foiled in this attempt by a Turkish patrol—they were returning to rejoin Auda's force when they came across a small Turkish post guarding a railway station some forty miles south of Amman. Taking the Turks by surprise and with the aid of some deadly accurate rifle fire, Lawrence's men took the station, set fire to the buildings and took their fill of loot from the dead and dying Turkish soldiery.

Lawrence's effort to distract the enemy's attention was not, however, altogether successful. As the march progressed they found that the Turks had blown up most of the wells on which Auda had counted to water his men and beasts. In an effort to prevent this "scorched earth" tactic, which threatened to bring his expedition to a dead stop, he sent an advance party on ahead to capture the wells at Aba el Lissan, his next staging post, which lay at the foot of the last mountain range between him and Akaba. The party did their job thoroughly, killing all the occupants of the Turkish guardhouse; but reports of the battle alerted every Turkish unit in the neighbourhood so that, when Auda and Lawrence got there, they found the entrance to the pass blocked by a Turkish battalion armed with artillery.

Fortunately the Turks had not taken the precaution of posting sentries, which blunder made it possible for Auda's men to clamber up the hillsides and, at a given signal, to open fire upon the Turkish troops camped in the mouth of the narrow gorge below. But in the scorching heat of this July morning, rifle barrels burned and blistered the toughest hands, and the shooting was sadly inaccurate and ineffective. Though safe enough in their mountain crevices from the frenzied volleys of shrapnel which the enfiladed Turks were loosing off in all directions, the Arabs were equally making no impression on the enemy. Furious with frustration, Auda flung at Lawrence, as a wild fusillade sputted harmlessly among the Turkish tents, "Well, how is it with the Howeitat? All talk and no work?" (This was a reference to the tearing he had had from Lawrence on the march for his boastful stories of bygone victories.)

"By God, indeed," Lawrence spat back at him, also infuriated that their advance should be thwarted by this unexpected enemy roadblock, "they shoot a lot and hit a little."

Auda tore off his head-cloth, threw it to the ground and ran off up the hill shouting to his men to follow him and get mounted. A few moments later, led by the old warrior, a force of fifty horsemen was charging at the bewildered Turkish infantry who swayed and finally broke in terror before the shrieking onslaught. Nasir had fortunately anticipated the wild old man's desperate move and, with Lawrence at his side, followed up in a flank attack with the rest of the camel force. The Turks were now in full retreat, a brown flood of demoralized humanity running and screaming as they were hit or ridden down by the horses and camels of their pursuers. Lawrence drove his camel forward, shrieking ecstatically at this sudden turn of fortune and firing his pistol wildly at the backs of the terrified scurrying column of enemy soldiers. Suddenly the beast collapsed in its tracks and fell dead beneath him. Lawrence was knocked unconscious by the fall. When he recovered his senses he discovered that he had shot the wretched animal through the head with his own revolver!

By this time, too, the battle was over. The Turks had lost three hundred dead and one hundred and sixty prisoners. Only a few of their gunners had got away and a handful of officers who had been able to grab horses to make their escape. Arab casualties were two dead. Auda came up to Lawrence bubbling over with pride and excitement and throwing back at his friend the taunts about the Howeitat's ability to fight and shoot. The old warrior had had a memorable day's fighting; his mare had been shot from under him, his clothes had been ripped by a Turkish volley, six bullets had passed through his robes, shattering his binoculars, his holster and his sword-scabbard; but he, Auda, had as always emerged victorious. Most of all, thanks to his furious gesture, the way to Akaba was now open.

In spite of the victory Lawrence was in no mood to enjoy Auda's boastings. From the captured Turkish tents where he sat, hardly hearing the old man telling and retelling of the day's deeds of valour, he could see the littered dead lying in clumps like so many ant-hills on the valley's floor. Then he rose and slowly walked towards the scene of carnage.

The dead men looked wonderfully beautiful. The night was shining gently down, softening them into new ivory. Turks were white-skinned on their clothed parts, much whiter than the Arabs; and these soldiers had been very young. Close round them lapped the dark wormwood, now heavy with dew, in which the ends of moonbeams sparkled like sea-spray. The corpses seemed flung so pitifully on the ground, huddled anyhow in low heaps.

Surely if straightened they would be comfortable at last. So I put them all in order, one by one, very wearied myself, and longing to be of these quiet ones, not of the restless, noisy, aching mob up the valley, quarrelling over the plunder, boasting of their speed and strength to endure God knew how many toils and pains of this sort; with death, whether we won or lost, waiting to end the history.

Thus Lawrence has described his own reactions to the first slaughter that he was called upon to witness. At this point he felt for the first time neither Britisher nor Arab, but a creature apart, not belonging to any camp, a spirit above the common tumult. Who knows what thoughts, even hallucinations, then possessed him? From the very beginning of his life he had been different; from the age of puberty he had resisted the normal temptations and desires of the body, his shame at his bastardy having turned into a revulsion towards such appetites; and now on the threshold of the Holy Land this new missionary for men's freedom found himself walking in the footsteps of the greatest of all saviours.

How had he got there, unless by some divine ordinance? He was no soldier, nor was he a great Arabist. He had no special hatred for the enemy, only for cruelty and oppression in all its forms. He felt apart from his British associates—indeed whenever possible he lived apart from them. He was equally not of the Arab race, however he might feel identified with their cause. Were then his driving ambition and his superhuman endurance implanted in him by some supernatural power? And if so for what purpose? Surely not to free men to butcher and plunder their fellows and leave them huddled in the grotesque agonies of death to feed some predatory bird of prey. His mission must be to preach and teach, to win battles by avoiding them, to save life not to destroy it. Yet here in this other Golgotha his utmost effort could do no more than make the dead more comfortable in death.

❖   ❖   ❖

That night was spent addressing letters to the local tribes informing them of the victory and inviting them to take prisoner any Turkish units in their neighbourhood. One of the captured Turkish officers was persuaded to write to the enemy garrisons along the rest of the route to Akaba suggesting that they surrender if they wished to save Turkish lives. Then, superstitiously fearing to stay any longer among the corpses of so many Turkish dead, Auda gave the order to march on. As the dawn broke over the green, well-watered slopes about the oasis of Aba el Lissan, the column presented a strange spectacle. Not only was each Turkish prisoner mounted on a camel, pillion fashion, behind his Arab captor, but more than half the force wore Turkish tunics over their robes, in accordance with the Arab custom of wearing the clothes of the defeated enemy as a mark of triumph in battle.

The device of warning letters to the local sheikhs and Turkish commanders paid off well. The first Turkish post they encountered had been taken by local Bedouin by the time they arrived and the second only put up a token resistance before surrendering. After this every post they came across had been abandoned, the enemy having fallen back on Akaba. And, with local tribes joining up every few miles in the hope of loot, Auda's force had more than doubled its numbers by the time they came in sight of their objective.

A few miles from Akaba, Auda, Nasir and Lawrence held a council of war in a windless gorge at the mouth of the Wadi Itm. Their agents had reported that the town was held by a garrison of only three hundred men who were short of food, but that the Turks would probably not surrender without a fight. Arguments swayed back and forth among the tribesmen, some for caution, others for boldness. The cautious urged a parley, the bold retorted that all of Akaba's defences faced the sea and that a small garrison could not hold an attack from the land. In the crush of hundreds of fiercely debating men, unwashed and sweat-soaked after nearly three weeks of marching in the summer heat, the stench became so overpowering that Lawrence broke up the council and announced that he would send the Turkish garrison a message under a flag of truce inviting them to surrender.

Disgruntled at this curtailment of their right of debate, the Arabs sulkily withdrew to await developments. These were as the bold had prophesied. The Turks fired upon the white flag party before they could reach the enemy lines. Next, Lawrence tried sending Turkish prisoners, but again the Turks replied with their rifles. Thereupon, led by Lawrence's own two impish bodyguards, Daud and Farraj, the Bedouin sent a hail of bullets at the enemy trenches and were only with difficulty made to cease fire by Nasir. A third attempt to parley bore more fruit, the Turks replying this time that they would surrender in two days, if no reinforcements had by then arrived from the north. Lawrence, Nasir and Auda decided to accept this. They knew that no relief would be forthcoming for the enemy, for they had learned from their prisoners that the battalion they had destroyed at Aba el Lissan was the only reinforcement that the Turks had in this area.

So, on 6th July, two months after leaving Wejh, Lawrence entered Akaba and with Nasir and Auda took the surrender of the Turkish garrison. He had covered some eight hundred miles, excluding his digression to Damascus, to reach an objective that lay only two hundred and fifty miles from his starting point. But this long and painful effort of circumnavigation proved to have been a stroke of genius. Akaba had twice before been occupied by the Allies, first by a French and later a British landing party, but in each case the Turks defending the hills above the town had driven the invaders back into the sea. By assaulting the town from behind on the landward side, Lawrence had caught the Turks facing the wrong way and unprepared to defend their position.

Lawrence's first and most pressing problem in Akaba was hunger. The food supply was all but exhausted and, added to the semi-starving townpeople, was now an assortment of Arab irregulars and tribesmen and Turkish prisoners numbering over two thousand empty stomachs. The town was in ruins, the result of Anglo-French naval bombardment, and there was no wireless communication available to call up supplies from Egypt. There was therefore nothing for it but for Lawrence himself to go by camel as fast as possible to Suez to summon a relief ship, a journey of a hundred and fifty miles across the waterless Sinai desert. This was a poor reward for all the suffering he had endured to get to Akaba. But Lawrence knew that the twenty thousand pounds which he had carried away from Wejh had been spent on the journey and in equipping the expedition from Wadi Sirhan; so there was no gold left to bribe the tribesmen to stay. If he did not get food and money quickly the Bedouin would melt away into the desert whence they had come and he would be left without an army to hold the prize that he had so skilfully won, still less to continue the march northwards in fulfilment of his ambitions.

Before Lawrence set off it was agreed that Auda should go to Guweira to cover the landward approaches to Akaba and establish guard-posts at Petra, the ancient and impregnable Nabatean capital twenty miles north of Akaba, and two other points commanding the mountain defiles. Nasir and the rest would set the town in a state of defence and guard the prisoners, whom hunger was beginning to make rebellious. With eight Howeitat tribesmen, an exhausted Lawrence then started on what must rank as one of even this remarkable man's most extraordinary feats of endurance. True, his march to the Hejaz railway north of Amman on the journey from Wadi Sirhan was covered in as fast a time; but on that occasion he was relatively fresh, whereas after Akaba he was physically and emotionally exhausted and weak from lack of food. Yet such was his determination to get word to Suez of his men's needs, and to Cairo of his own success, that he covered the hundred and fifty miles in forty-nine hours with only one stop for water.

Lawrence reached the British post at Shatt on the Asian side of the Canal opposite Suez only to find it abandoned. Finding a telephone with some difficulty, he called British headquarters at Suez to ask for a boat to take him across the canal. A bored bureaucrat replied that he had no authority to comply with this request, Shatt had been abandoned because of plague and headquarters could not help. Lawrence was told he should try the Inland Water Board. But they were sorry they had no boats free for the moment. They would see what they could do next day. Lawrence lost his temper. The thought of having got so near to a little civilization like a bath and some clean clothes, after riding for four months in the desert, and then being forced by a handful of bureaucrats to stay in a plague-infested village was more than he could bear. After two more ineffectual calls, the operator finally took pity on him and connected him with the Embarkation Officer who, to Lawrence's joy and relief, turned out to be an old army friend.

❖   ❖   ❖

At Suez Lawrence took the train for Ismailia where, while waiting for his connection to Cairo, he saw Admiral Wemyss, who was on his way to Suez accompanied by some other important-looking brass hats. This was an opportunity not to be missed to make sure that the supplies he had asked for at Suez would in fact be sent to Akaba. But seeing and meeting the admiral were two very different things, for Lawrence, in spite of his recent bath, still looked in his travel-worn robes and sandals like any local beggar—at least to the little cluster of staff officers huddled about Wemyss and his high-ranking friends.

"Stand back there, you!" said a large perspiring figure in execrable Arabic, with red tabs on his khaki lapels. Then when Lawrence objected in English that he wished to speak to Admiral Wemyss, "What are you? A bloody Montenegrin dragoon?"

Lawrence responded amid the general laughter, "A staff captain in the army of the Sherif of Mecca."

"Meccan army! Bah! Never heard of it!" scoffed the damp-faced major.

"You will very soon," Lawrence softly replied.

At that moment Wemyss turned round and caught sight of Lawrence. Remembering still vividly the incident when he had refused to allow a British officer to board his ship in Arab dress, he recognized his erstwhile guest immediately.

"You again!" he said, but his tone was friendly as Lawrence, forgetting as usual to salute, passed within the rigid circle of the admiral's astonished escort with outstretched hand to tell his story.

"Splendid!" was the admiral's comment when he had finished. Then, "I'll send H.M.S. *Dufferin* with a load of food right away and she can bring back your prisoners. No need to consult Allenby about this."

"Allenby?" Lawrence stammered. "What's he doing here?"

"Oh, he's in command now. Murray's gone home."

12

Lawrence had not long to wait before he was summoned to see the new Commander-in-Chief. In Cairo he received a hero's welcome. He was promoted to major, recommended for the Order of the Bath, and, ironically enough, awarded the French Croix de Guerre. Colonel Clayton forgot his insubordination in careering off on his own, contrary to orders, and agreed without demur to send gold and anything else to Akaba that this brash young adventurer wanted sent. He also brought Lawrence up to date on the progress, or lack of it, in the Egyptian theatre of operations. Murray had been sent home after his second offensive against Gaza had failed with a casualty list of nearly six thousand. But, with Allenby, a new hope had arisen, for he was getting large reinforcements of men and guns. Allenby, too, was a cavalry soldier and believed in a war of mobility. As such, Clayton thought, he promised to bring a refreshingly new and lively mind to bear upon the war against the Turks and would be a more understanding and co-operative C.-in-C. to the Arabs than his predecessor or anyone in Murray's entourage.

Lawrence was certainly not disappointed with his first encounter with Allenby. Bouncing into the room dressed in his Arab robes, and treating the Commander-in-Chief as he might have some contemporary who had asked him to drop in for a drink, he must have been the strangest army officer that the General had ever received. Lawrence's own picture of the scene is frank and graphic.

It was a comic interview, for Allenby was physically large and confident, and morally so great that the comprehension of our littleness came slow to him. He sat in his chair looking at me—not straight, as his custom was, but sideways, puzzled . . . he was hardly prepared for anything so odd as myself —a little bare-footed silk-skirted man offering to hobble his enemy by his preaching if given stores and arms and a fund of two hundred thousand sovereigns to convince and control his converts. Allenby could not make out how much was genuine performer and how much charlatan. The problem was working behind his eyes, and I left him unhelped to solve it. . . . At the end he put up his chin and said quite directly, "Well, I will do for you what I can," and that ended it.

Lawrence comments that he learned that what Allenby could do "was enough for his very greediest servant."

This account is interesting not only because it describes the first encounter between these two men, who were destined to play the principal and indispensable rôles in the defeat of the Ottoman empire, nor merely because of what it reveals of the straightforwardness coupled with insight that were Allenby's chief characteristics: it is even more interesting because of what it reveals of Lawrence himself. "How much was genuine performer and how much charlatan?" Perhaps Lawrence did not help Allenby to find out because he himself did not know the answer to the question. Certainly he must have asked himself this question at the time. For, according to his own account, he was continually plagued with the knowledge that had come to him of the true intentions behind the Sykes-Picot agreement.

Yet the remarkable fact is that there is no suggestion that Lawrence seriously contemplated abandoning his mission at this stage. On the contrary; soliloquizing in retrospect upon this period, Lawrence says:

. . . not being a perfect fool, I could see that, if we won the war, the promises to the Arabs were dead paper. Had I been an honourable adviser I would have sent my men home, and not let them risk their lives for such stuff. Yet the Arab inspiration was our main tool in winning the Eastern war. So I assured them that England kept her word in letter and spirit . . . but, of course . . . I was continually bitter and ashamed.

Lawrence not only reassured the Arabs when rumours of the fraud reached their ears; he went right ahead in Cairo to plan and to argue the next moves in the Arab campaign, suggesting to Clayton that the capture of Akaba had earned him the right to a free hand in his job as liaison officer with the Arab command independent of the orders of his British superiors, Joyce and Newcombe. More important still, he proposed that Feisal's army should become the right wing of Allenby's forces and should be under British supreme command. For this purpose Feisal should be detached from Sherifian control and move his base from Wejh, which had become a backwater, to Akaba, which was to be the supply centre for the advance northwards into Syria. Save for the fact that Joyce was appointed nominal commander of Akaba, all these requests from Lawrence were met in full by Allenby and the General Staff.

How is it that a man, so enmeshed in the Arab movement and so identified with the Arab peoples, could have gone ahead so light-heartedly with these dispositions in the face of such evidence of Allied perfidy and not decided to "send his men home," refusing to let "them risk their lives for such stuff"? Perhaps the "genuine performer" felt that, come what may, he must fulfil his mission and that, after Akaba, the Arabs were capable not only of fighting together in war but of standing together in victory to assert their rights and enforce fulfilment of the pledges that had been made to them. And the "charlatan" saw the Arab inspiration as the "main tool" for gaining his own personal ambition to be the power behind the throne of a new Arab empire. Like many other men in the pages of history, when faced simultaneously with a grave moral challenge and a great material opportunity, Lawrence's reactions were ambivalent. Where he is unique is that the debate about him still continues and nobody has ever proved conclusively which side of his nature was the dominant force.

It is only fair to say that treachery and intrigue were not by any means an Allied monopoly at this time. While Lawrence was in Jidda getting Hussein's agreement to the attachment of Feisal's army to the British command, evidence reached him from Cairo that Auda was in treasonable correspondence with the Turks. Hastening to Guweira he good-humouredly confronted the Howeitat chief and his cousin Mohammed with proof of this treachery. Auda admitted that he had written to the Turkish governor of Maan offering, in return for arms and cash, to desert the Sherifian cause. He had done so because he was angry at getting no personal reward from the British for the capture of Akaba and was disappointed that no guns or troops had been sent to support him. All this had suggested the need for a little reinsurance policy with the enemy. But, when Lawrence told him of Feisal's impending move to Akaba and of Allenby's plans to send guns, rifles, explosives and money to the new base, he readily agreed to break off his Turkish contacts and to co-operate in the future only with the Allies.

No one could have handled this difficult situation with greater skill or understanding than Lawrence. Any other officer would probably have got angry and raged at Auda for ingratitude or lack of faith. But Lawrence was too steeped in Arab thinking to take a high and mighty self-righteous attitude. Besides his own sense of fraudulence in his relations with the Arabs probably inhibited any tendency to indignation that he might have felt at this case of Arab intrigue. Instead of blustering, therefore, Lawrence adopted a teasing line with Auda and succeeded in making him laugh at his own stupidity in believing himself abandoned by his allies and in thinking that he could have such dealings with the enemy without being found out.

Inevitably the encounter ended with a banquet at which Auda, his face gleaming with the hot wet fat of a freshly killed sheep, recited interminably the well-embroidered tale of his wild charge that routed the Turks at Aba el Lissan.

"Sixteen bullet holes in my robes," he declaimed, "and two of my mares shot dead under me."

"Last time you told it, it was twenty-six bullets and three mares killed," Lawrence twitted him. Then they all laughed and Lawrence went on his way back to Akaba to telephone to Cairo and reassure Clayton that all was well at Guweira "and no treachery abroad." Lawrence admits that he deliberately misled his superiors in this report but he felt it imperative to keep them confident "and ourselves a legend." They would not have understood Auda's motives and, in their own interests, it was better to conceal from them the truth.

13

The capture of Akaba had closed the Hejaz war and the next task was to make this important Red Sea port a secure and effective base for the advance northwards which was to coincide with Allenby's plans for a general offensive along the entire Allied front before the end of 1917. To this end Akaba became a teeming hive of activity. Feisal's army arrived from Wejh in a fleet of transports; armoured cars came in from Suez; Egyptian troops, Algerian troops, British officers, French officers poured in with guns, machineguns, high explosives, small arms and ammunition until the hastily constructed jetties nearly collapsed beneath the weight of tramping feet and packing cases piled to perilous heights. A landing ground was laid out, roads were built to speed up communications between the port and its defence perimeter beyond the coastal hills and the defence posts at Guweira and Petra were reinforced with mountain guns and machine-guns. Akaba became in short a bristling fortress within a matter of six weeks after its capture.

But the Allies were not alone in their activity and preparations. The Turks, smarting under their recent defeat, were also making ready—to recapture Akaba. This was of critical importance for two reasons. First, to teach the Arabs who was master in Arabia and to discourage adherents to the Sherifian cause among the northern tribes. Second, to deny to the Allies the use of this vital supply base for an offensive against Jerusalem and Syria, which they rightly assumed Allenby had been sent out to get going. By the middle of August the Turks had reinforced their garrison at Maan with six thousand infantry, a regiment of cavalry and of mounted infantry and a squadron of aircraft equipped with bombs. Two battalions of infantry were sent to Aba el Lissan, which the Arabs had left undefended. Though the enemy suffered constantly from the pin-pricks of Arab attacks on their patrols and supply transports, they were not dislodged. On the contrary; they seemed to be consolidating for a major assault through the same mountain route that the Arabs had used to capture Akaba.

Lawrence decided that the moment had come to break up this threatening concentration and asked Allenby for aircraft to do the job. A flight of biplane bombers was immediately sent to operate from the new airstrip. Their commander, Captain Stent, and his fellow pilots were a dare-devil band, experienced in low-level bombing and the art of forced landings in the desert. First, they went to work on Maan where they dropped thirty-two bombs on the railway station, the barracks, the aerodrome and even, so Lawrence claims, the Turkish General's kitchen, where they "finished his cook and his breakfast" and inflicted heavy casualties and damage on the enemy's own bomber aircraft. The following day they twice attacked Turkish concentrations at Aba el Lissan, going in at zero feet and scattering men, horses and guns in a screaming pandemonium of destruction at point-blank range.

When they had recovered from these raids, the Turks decided to attack before further damage to morale and material caught up with them. Curiously enough they chose as their objective Petra, which, guarded by defiles so narrow that two camels could hardly move along them side by side, was an impregnable fortress, if properly defended—and Lawrence had seen to it that old Maulud was posted there with a couple of hundred Arab regulars and plenty of machine-guns. The Turks lost an entire company in this action and were forced to withdraw without making the slightest impression on the defenders of the ancient city, perched high out of sight among the towering red rocks above the famous gorge, which became a death-trap to the invaders.

The Turkish threat to Akaba had been halted; but Lawrence decided that one more blow must be struck at the enemy to complete his demoralization. Clearly the Hejaz railway was indicated for this, but where exactly should it be cut to inflict the utmost damage? North of Maan would seem to have been the natural choice so as to interrupt the build-up of Turkish forces from Damascus and Aleppo. But here Lawrence was faced with difficulties. He had been able to bring off his diversionary attack on the railway north of Amman during the march from Wadi Sirhan, because Auda's main force had been fairly close at hand and because the local tribes had been well conditioned by propaganda and could be relied upon to let the raiding party pass without hindrance through their territory. But the latest reports showed that the effect of this propaganda had worn off and that the Turks were making some headway with a new and subtle line of argument, insinuating that Feisal had sold out to the infidel Christians and was but the tool of Anglo-French machinations. The Turks had themselves got wind of the Sykes-Picot treaty and were using their knowledge to some effect. Some of the Sherifian troops on their way to reinforce Feisal had mutinied and refused to leave the Hejaz. Even the court of the Grand Sherif was not immune to these wedge-driving tactics of the enemy and the rift that came at the end of the war in the relations between Feisal and his father and brothers was probably first opened at about this time.

To attack the railway so far to the north without local support would have required a larger force than Lawrence felt would be justified. He could not denude the Akaba garrison for a railway raid, however important. He therefore decided to content himself with an attack on Mudauwra station, about eighty miles

east of Akaba—an important target because it was
the only water post for several hundred miles along
the desert railway. For the raid he selected two
sergeants, an Australian and a Britisher, whom he
called Lewis and Stokes after the machine-guns and
mortar which were their weapons for the trip, a sheikh
in Feisal's entourage called Aid, and a dozen or so of
the Emir's soldiers and cameleers to carry the explosives. For escort he relied on Howeitat tribesmen
whom he picked up at Guweira on the way.

The route to Mudauwra lay through the Wadi
Rumm, a long broad valley bounded by sheer cliffs
of red rock a thousand or more feet high. Lawrence
described his passage through this magnificent piece
of Grand Canyon country in these words:

> The ascent became gentle, till the valley was a
> confined tilted plain. The hills on the right grew
> taller and sharper, a fair counterpart of the other
> side which straightened itself to one massive ram-
> part of redness. . . . They were not unbroken walls
> of rock, but were built sectionally, in crags like
> gigantic buildings, along the two sides of their
> street. . . . The crags were capped in nests of domes,
> less hotly red than the body of the hill; rather grey
> and shallow. They gave the finishing semblance of
> Byzantine architecture to this irresistible place; this
> processional way greater than imagination. The
> Arab armies would have been lost in the length
> and breadth of it, and within the walls a squadron
> of aeroplanes could have wheeled in formation.
> Our little caravan grew self-conscious, and fell dead
> quiet, afraid and ashamed to flaunt its smallness in
> the presence of the stupendous hills.

It was not long before Lawrence's attentions were
brought back with a jolt from admiring all this
grandeur to coping once more with a threatening tribal
situation. Aid had gone blind in the heat and glare
of the sun. Lawrence, fearing to take him along on

the raid so handicapped, decided to escort him to
some Bedouins camped to the south of Rumm. The
September heat had in any case worn out some of
the pack camels and fresh beasts were needed to carry
the explosives. But the Bedouin whom they found
turned out to be from tribes who were highly resentful
of Auda, whom they suspected of seeking to take
them over. Lawrence had only recently had to quell
another incipient rebellion among some Howeitat
sheikhs in Guweira who were threatening to walk out
on Auda unless he gave them their due share of the
gold that he had got from the British. But the tribesmen at Rumm proved tougher nuts to crack than the
sheikhs and he spent an uneasy night after a bitter
argument conducted at a temperature of 120 degrees
in the shade, and the shade "was a surge of flies."

The following day Auda's nephew, Zaal, arrived to
join Lawrence, and after skilfully playing the tribesmen off against each other, they managed to get the
recalcitrants to pledge their support on condition that
an emissary of Feisal would be sent to guarantee
their independence from Auda. This was accomplished, although it involved the unfortunate Lawrence in a ride back to Akaba to ask the Emir to
send a mediator with him to Rumm, and on 16th
September the tribesmen and the raiders rode on
together to Mudauwra. But it was an unhappy disunited force that set out from Rumm, driven more
by the prospect of loot than by any sense of
camaraderie. Zaal and Feisal's mediator, Sheikh
Abdulla el Feir, had prevailed in argument but they
had not fully convinced the tribesmen; and it was
only the untiring diplomacy of Lawrence during the
first day's march that produced any semblance of
harmony in the ranks when they camped that night
within sight of their target.

A reconnaissance after dark showed that the station was more strongly held than they expected and
that their little band of a hundred and twenty would
be greatly outnumbered by the defending Turks. Law-

rence therefore decided to give the station itself a
miss but to find a place somewhere down the line to
lay a mine and blow up the first train that came
along. Here they were in luck in finding a railway
bridge, where they could plant their explosive where
it would do the utmost damage and where also was
excellent cover for ambushing the Turks as they
spilled out of the derailed train. Lawrence laid the
charges while Lewis and Stokes set up their mortar
and machine-gun nests on rock ledges overlooking
the track.

About noon the following day the watchman
shouted from his vantage point in the hills above
Lawrence's camp that a train was approaching. Order-
ing each man to his action station, Lawrence waited
until the engine was right on top of the bridge before
signalling to Salem, Feisal's best slave, to whom had
been assigned the honour of pressing the plunger. A
tremendous roar followed and train and track were
temporarily lost to sight in a cloud of black dust and
smoke; then the shattering crash and rending of steel
ripping into steel and wood splintering against wood;
and then for a leaden moment, silence. After which
pandemonium broke loose. Lawrence's machine-guns
clattered into action and Bedouins began firing volleys
at the dismembered train, while the Turks were mown
down as fast as they poured out from the derailed
coaches. Then above the whine and chatter of rifle
and Lewis-gun fire came the crash of two mortar
shells carefully aimed to finish off the only small group
of Turkish soldiers who had been able to escape from
the death-trap of the train and stage a counter-attack
from behind some rocks.

As the few survivors of the mortar's explosion
broke cover and ran, the Arabs went berserk, hurling
themselves upon the train and tearing it to pieces.

The valley [Lawrence records] was a weird
sight. The Arabs, gone raving mad, were rushing
about at top speed, bare-headed and half naked,

screaming, shooting into the air, clawing one another nail and fist, while they burst open trucks and staggered back and forward with immense bales, which they ripped by the rail-side, and tossed through, smashing what they did not want. . . . There were scores of carpets spread about; dozens of mattresses and flowered quilts, blankets in heaps, clothes for men and women in full variety; clocks, cooking-pots, food, ornaments and weapons. To one side stood thirty or forty hysterical women, unveiled; tearing their clothes and hair, shrieking themselves distracted. The Arabs without regard to them went on wrecking the household goods; looting their absolute fill. Camels had become common property. Each man frantically loaded the nearest with what it could carry and shooed it westward into the void, while he turned to his next fancy.

Once again, as at Aba el Lissan when the Arabs were boasting of the Turks they had killed and the booty they had plundered, Lawrence was overwhelmed by the desire to detach himself from so much slaughter and pillage. Turning his back upon the scene, he walked across to where the last Turkish defenders had fallen and set about straightening and arranging their corpses. Some wore a peaceful expression, others an agonized grimace as if scandalized by the savage, shrieking and grotesque antics of the looters.

Then, as suddenly as it had begun, the tumult ceased and an eerie silence descended upon the valley. Lawrence looked round to find that he, Zaal and the two sergeants were alone with the few prisoners who had survived the action. The Bedouins had vanished into the desert with their booty. As they struggled back to Akaba, harried by a Turkish column which had set out from Mudauwra in pursuit of the raiders, Lawrence reflected that "victory always undid an Arab force."

❖   ❖   ❖

Back in Feisal's headquarters Lawrence was now renowned, not only as the man who could get limitless guns and gold for the Sherifian cause, but even more as a corsair supreme, a desert pirate and guerilla leader of the utmost daring and cool courage, whose appearance in an Arab camp would be greeted with joyous and admiring cries of *"El Aurens, El Aurens"* and a rush of eager brown humanity reaching out to touch their hero's robes. Also the sight of his Bedouin followers returning with camels scarcely able to stagger beneath a weight of booty sufficient to enrich a whole tribe had excited the greatest envy throughout Feisal's army. Stories of the Mudauwra mining raid and the loot brought home spread like a bush-fire across the desert, though not always with strict accuracy. Witness the Beni Atiyeh tribe who wrote to Feisal, saying, "send us a laurens and we will blow up trains with it."

The flame of revolt began to blaze again, where it had burned low since the fall of Akaba, and those who had not yet been touched by Feisal's message became enthused by the wild tales that came from his camp. Lawrence, realizing the importance of this new source of inspiration, planned further raids on the Hejaz railway. Profiting from the reviving activism of the tribes in the north, he switched his attentions to the Maan sector and in the next four months destroyed seventeen locomotives and hundreds of coaches and wagons.

This was a bad blow for the Turks, for it struck against morale as well as materials. The engine-drivers went on strike and civilian traffic between Damascus and the Hejaz almost ceased altogether. "Travelling became an uncertain terror for the enemy." The loss of rolling stock made it impossible for the enemy to withdraw their Medina garrison to reinforce the Palestine front and began to hinder their manoeuvrability around Jerusalem at the very moment when the British armies were gathering for their November offensive. So, when word reached him in mid-October that Allenby wished to discuss the Arab army's part in his plans to break out of Gaza, Lawrence hastened to G.H.Q. flushed with pride in his achievements.

14

Once again Lawrence bounced into Allenby's office, a jaunty cock-sparrow swathed in Bedouin robes. But this time Allenby was not in a mood to let his visitor show off. The Commander-in-Chief had serious business on his hands and his time was strictly rationed. Coming straight to the point he asked Lawrence what his railway raids meant, "or rather whether they meant anything beyond the melodramatic advertisement of Feisal's cause."

The unexpected shaft pricked the bubble of Lawrence's pride and left him replying defensively that his purpose was to leave the Hejaz railway working just enough to keep Fakhri's Turks in Medina where they would be "fed at less cost than if in Prison in Cairo." This did not satisfy Allenby, who was thinking in altogether more ambitious terms. He wanted plans to be made for a general Arab uprising in the north when he launched his attack on the Gaza-Beersheba line.

Lawrence pondered the proposal silently. He was greatly tempted to fall in with it. He knew that he could probably take Deraa, between Amman and Damascus, with the aid of the local Arab tribes; and Deraa was, as he put it, "the navel of the Turkish armies in Syria." As the junction of the Jerusalem-Haifa-Damascus-Medina railways, it was the focal point of every front; and Lawrence knew that the tribes in this area were good fighting men, "educated and armed by Feisal from Akaba." What was more, their leaders were repeatedly urging Feisal to give the word to deliver Deraa.

Yet Lawrence hesitated and, after reflection, declined Allenby's proposition. The reason he afterwards gave was that he felt he could not be sure of the British army and its "untried" commander successfully breaking through at Gaza and that, since the tribes could only rise once, it was asking them to undertake too great a hazard. In fact a more likely reason was, as he also reflected, that "such an exploit would have done the Allenby business, but was not one which Feisal could scrupulously afford, unless he had a hope of then establishing himself there." Lawrence did not want Deraa, the gateway to Damascus, to be taken by anyone but Feisal, his chosen nominee to occupy the throne of Syria and to realize his Arabian dream.

Lawrence commented that, on this visit to G.H.Q., he felt torn between his two masters, Feisal and Allenby, and not for the first time. But it is fairly clear that he had for several months cast his lot with the Emir and would put his interests before anyone else's. The fact that, in the main, Feisal's interests coincided with the Allies' was fortunate indeed for the conduct of the campaign against the Turks. But there can be little doubt that Lawrence would not at any stage have hesitated to sacrifice the wider benefit to realize the claims of his chosen king, justifying himself—with some reason—by his knowledge that the Allies fully intended to sacrifice Feisal when they had finished with his services.

As a compromise and to keep Allenby well-disposed to the Arab cause, Lawrence suggested that he take a raiding party to destroy the railway viaduct over the Yarmuk river, between Deraa and the Sea of Galilee. This would involve a most hazardous march of more than four hundred miles behind the Turkish lines; but, if the bridge could be blown up, the enemy's only means of communication would be cut between his bases in the north and Palestine and cut for months, since the viaduct spanned a very deep gorge and could not be rebuilt without great difficulty.

Allenby accepted the scheme and told Lawrence to get going as soon as possible. He wanted the bridge blown a few days after his main offensive opened in the first week of November. With great speed the expedition was got ready, Feisal agreeing to release Ali ibn el Hussein to take the place of Sherif Nasir, who was not available. A sheikh of the Harith (not to be confused with the Emir Ali, Hussein's eldest son) who had shared in Feisal's captivity in Damascus, Ali was a highly enthusiastic expert in the joyous art of demolition. Courageous, resourceful and energetic, he loved dangerous exploits and brought to them the added advantage of titanic physical strength. He could rise from a kneeling position on the ground with a man sitting on the palm of each hand and he could run beside a trotting camel on his bare feet for half a mile and then leap into the saddle. He was a man after Lawrence's heart and the Yarmuk expedition was just his type of adventure. Besides, he was a relative of the Beni Sakhr chiefs through whose territory the raiders would have to march.

Lawrence's plan was to ride to Azrak, about two hundred and fifty miles north-east of Akaba, and establish a base there from which to attack the Yarmuk bridge once he was assured of sufficient local support. The question presented some difficulties. The Serahin around Azrak would probably co-operate loyally enough, so the latest intelligence reports suggested, but there was no guarantee of the tribes around the objective which was another one hundred and fifty miles further on. Nuri Shaalan's Ruwalla had retired to their winter quarters hundreds of miles away and their summer neighbours, the Beni Hassan, were an unknown quantity.

While Lawrence was pondering this problem, an apparent windfall occurred which suggested a solution. A few days before his expedition was to leave Akaba an Algerian Emir, Abd el Kader el Jazairi, arrived to join Feisal. Abd el Kader's family had a distinguished record of service to the cause of Arab independence. His grandfather had defended Algiers against the French and his brother had been recently martyred by the Turks. Like his dead brother, the Emir had been living in exile in Syria, whence he claimed to have escaped after some hair-raising adventures. To Lawrence he seemed half mad with religious fanaticism and his escape story did not ring at all true—it was later discovered that the Turks were using him as a double agent—but his usefulness lay in the fact that he promised the support of his fellow Algerian exiles who lived in the Yarmuk river valley. Besides, Feisal, though admitting his insanity, thought him honest. Since the only warning of his likely treachery had come from Bremond, Lawrence dismissed it as French prejudice and took the Algerian along on the trip—a grave mistake, as things turned out, for Abd el Kader was to desert his companons at a moment of great peril, having done nothing to help and everything to upset their plans.

❖   ❖   ❖

On 24th October the expedition left Akaba. Apart from Ali and Abd el Kader, it included a British sapper officer named Wood who was a specialist in explosives, Lawrence's personal bodyguard, which now numbered six, and a handful of machine-gunners of the Indian cavalry. For the Bedouin fighting force that would be needed to protect them while they blew the viaduct, Lawrence decided to rely on what he could raise from Azrak, rather than encumber himself with a large detachment for the long slog northwards.

From the very start things went wrong. Wood, unaccustomed to desert travel and handicapped by a bullet wound in the head that he had collected in France, got sick with dysentery; Ali and Abd el Kader fell out with one another and were only kept from quarrelling openly by Lawrence being in constant attendance; the Indians could not manage the camels; and, while crossing the Hejaz railway south of Maan on the way to Auda's camp, the expedition met with an unexpected Turkish patrol, which further delayed their progress. Worst of all, when they found Auda camped in his winter quarters near Jefer, the old man was rowing again with the Howeitat sheikhs about money and regretfully declined Lawrence's invitation to join in the raid. Zaal also refused, having, as Lawrence observed, become softened by the acquisition of riches from the summer raids. Then to cap everything, Auda, as he embraced his English friend and wished him God's peace on his journey, whispered through his black beard, "Beware of Abd el Kader."

Thoroughly depressed by these setbacks and upset by the warning that he was nursing a traitor to his bosom on a journey already hazardous enough in itself, Lawrence pushed on to the wells of Bair to try his luck with Ali's tribal relatives, the Beni Sakhr. Then a few moments after his departure the noise of distant thunder came to him upon a sudden gust of the west wind. With a shout of joy, he turned his camel to ride back down the labouring column, proclaiming that Allenby's offensive had started and that the hated Turks were now being driven back by the murderous fire of British guns. Ali spontaneously joined in the general rejoicing but, as soon as Lawrence was out of hearing, Abd el Kader hissed in his ear, "I see no reason for gladness. These are fellow Moslems caught in the deadly rain of the infidel's guns."

Sheikh Ali kept his silence and said not a word to Lawrence about the Algerian's comment. Things had so far gone badly, it was true, but they would soon be among his friends and there they would find loyal support. Indeed, when they reached Bair exactly a week from their starting date, their luck seemed to have turned. A royal welcome met them, with the entire Beni Sakhr tribe turning out to receive them with cheers and shouts, galloping wildly round the camp, shooting their rifles into the air and calling upon Allah to give strength to Ali and *El Aurens* to deliver them from their Turkish oppressors.

The display aroused a ferocious jealousy in Abd el Kader who, after vainly trying to attract attention to himself like a child ignored in favour of another, sat and sulked in the chieftain's tent during the whole course of the inevitable banquet that followed after sunset. As the welcome sound of Allenby's guns grew louder, his mood became more and more morose. Nor was he any better-tempered when on the following morning the expedition set off for Azrak accompanied by Sheikh Mifleh of the Beni Sakhr, their host of the previous evening, and twenty of his toughest warriors. Clearly the Algerian Emir was concocting some treachery and Lawrence and Ali wore troubled faces as the column wound its way northwards. Only the desert tradition of *rafiq* prevented an open conflict breaking out between Ali and Abd el Kader. Though filled by now with dislike and distrust of his associate, Ali had pledged himself to the Algerian as his ally and brother in battle and this bond must be honoured, according to Bedouin lore, until the battle was over and he was released from his pact of non-aggression. Not even a suspicion amounting almost to a certainty that the other was contemplating some gross betrayal was excuse for drawing his sword against his sworn ally.

15

The rest of the four days' march to Azrak brought a mixture of developments, mostly bad. On the credit side they were joined by two sheikhs of the Zebn Sukhur tribe, Fahad and Adhub. These two were brothers and famous fighters. Fahad was a melancholy silent type with a trim appearance and "tragic eyes," Adhub was his opposite, noisy and uncouth with a snub nose and "gleaming green eyes flickering hungrily from object to object." Then just as they were approaching Azrak they met a large group of the Serahin who were on their way to join Feisal. This seemed to be a real stroke of good luck, for it was to the Serahin that Lawrence had all along thought he would have to look to guide and guard his demolition party from Azrak to the Yarmuk bridge. But his initial rejoicing was soon cut short. After the evening meal was over they outlined their plan of action to the Paramount Sheikh, an old toothless character called Mteir. He would have none of it. The bridge could not be blown, he asserted. For one thing, the whole area was alive with Turks. For another, he distrusted the villagers in the neighbourhood—Abd el Kader's Algerian exiles.

Lawrence saw that he was in great trouble. If the Serahin stayed in their tents he would have to fail Allenby with incalculable consequences upon the future of British aid to Feisal. He brought in Ali, Fahad, Mifleh and Adhub to support his efforts to talk round Mteir and the Serahin sheikhs.

We put it to them [he wrote] not abstractly, but concretely, for their case, how life in mass was sensual only, to be lived and loved in its extremity. There could be no rest-houses for revolt, no dividend of joy paid out. Its spirit was accretive, to endure as far as the sense would endure and to use each such advance as base for further adventure, deeper deprivation, sharper pain. Sense could not reach back or forward. A felt emotion was a conquered emotion, an experience gone dead, which we buried by expressing it.

In the end the force of his argument prevailed and the Serahin were talked or shamed into lending themselves to the raiding party. Lawrence decided to waste no further time and, after a night of rest amidst the ruins of the old crusader castle that was all that remained of Azrak, pressed on to his objective. Allenby's offensive had now been in progress for five days and he had to make haste if he was to keep to the agreed time-table. A few hours before his departure he discovered that Abd el Kader had disappeared. Since it was obvious from the warnings of his leanings towards the Turks and from his behaviour on the march that he had gone to alert the enemy about the plans for the Yarmuk raid, Lawrence at once took counsel with Ali and Fahad. But these two were not the type to give up easily, and, though Lawrence admitted that "it was not a confident decision," they agreed to take a gamble on the probable incompetence and slowness of the Turkish reaction. With a great effort they could march the rest of the eighty miles to their objective before dawn the next day, though this gave them only thirteen hours to cover the journey.

Lawrence then made his dispositions for the final trek and assault; but Abd el Kader's treachery had unnerved him and only his determination to be no less daring than the headstrong Ali kept him going. Choosing the fastest camels and the best fighting men from

the Beni Sakhr and Serahin, he decided to rush the
bridge silently before dawn with a small party and
then, directly the demolition job was done, to escape
into the hills and back to Azrak as fast as possible.

To begin with the plan seemed to work surprisingly
well. Though they met a couple of Turkish patrols on
the way, they had no difficulty in keeping out of sight
and the only disturbance they met was a shepherd
boy, who mistook them for outlaws bent on stealing
his sheep and fired in terror upon them as they
passed. When they reached the bridge at Tel el She-
hab in a drizzling rain, the Turkish sentries betrayed
no sign that Abd el Kader's presumed treachery had
yet alerted them to any extra vigilance.

Silently and with the utmost care, the Indian machine-gunners and the Bedouins carrying the explosives unloaded their precious cargoes from the backs
of the pack camels. The only sound in the still moon-
less night came from the rushing torrent of the river
gorge hundreds of feet below their rocky bivouac.
Wood took charge of the Indians whose job was to
cover Lawrence, Ali, Fahad and their Arab porters
while they placed the explosives under the viaduct. In
single file the demolition party crept forward through
the slippery rocks down to the point where the bridge
girders stretched naked and inviting before them. A
few yards from where they crouched noiselessly, a
Turkish sentry paced leisurely up and down the
metals of the track. With a whispered curse Lawrence motioned to Fahad to move on to another hiding place from where they could fix their explosives
to the girders without being seen by the sentry. Then,
just as the two had started to crawl away, one of the
Arabs carrying the explosives dropped his rifle. As it
clanged on the rocks the sentry sounded the alarm
and started firing wildly in the direction of the sound.
The Arabs, unable to restrain themselves, fired back
betraying their position in the crevices of the deep
ravine. The Turkish guard-post, summoned by the
sentry's alarm, then concentrated their fire on the

Arabs who, when the bullets began to spatter close to their sacks of gelignite, promptly hurled most of them into the river for fear that they might explode and kill them. There was nothing to do now but run for it as fast as possible. Scrambling and cursing their way back up the steep crags of the ravine, Lawrence and the Arabs rejoined the main party, mounted their camels and headed for Azrak. The raid had failed; and, to make matters even worse, on the way back some of the Serahin, disgruntled at its failure and the absence of loot, waylaid a party of villagers returning from Deraa and robbed them. This provoked reprisals from other Arabs living in the neighbourhood and made the retreat an even sorrier and angrier affair. The sound of Allenby's guns still thundering at the Turkish lines away to the south added a further reminder of his failure to the embittered Lawrence.

Even an attempt to work off their outraged feelings by blowing up a train on their return seemed to be jinxed. Using a reserve bag of gelignite Lawrence laid the charges under the metals and with Ali and the Arabs lay in wait to ambush the wreck. But when he depressed the plunger nothing happened and the train rumbled unharmed over the dynamited section. It was full of Turkish troops going to reinforce the Palestine front and, as it panted past him, Lawrence realized suddenly that he was in full view of the enemy who were peering at him through field glasses. Having expected the plunger to work, he had not bothered to seek proper cover and, to save himself from further investigation by the Turks, he now had to put on a ridiculous act of waving to the passing enemy, while his Arab friends looked on furiously from their hiding places. On rejoining Ali and the ambush party, Sheikh Mifleh accused him of deliberately letting the train go by and the Arabs shook their heads and talked with foreboding of the "evil eye" being upon them. When Lawrence chided them for their timidity they became furious and attacked him bitterly. Ali defended him nobly, although shivering with fever and thoroughly miserable with the cold rain that had set in. The Prophet had given the Sherifs such as himself the faculty of "sight," he asserted, and he could see that their luck would now turn for the better. This quieted the enraged Arabs and gave Lawrence a breathing-space to fix the faulty exploder.

Placing his charges in the same position on the track Lawrence sat down to await the next train. It turned out to be a magnificent target, with two locomotives and carrying no less a passenger than Jemal Pasha himself, who was hastening to defend Jerusalem against Allenby's advance. With a tremendous explosion the first locomotive blew up as the charge went off underneath it. But Lawrence was hit by a flying fragment of metal and, as firing broke out on all sides, fell right between the two fires. Ali and some twenty Beni Sakhr ran to his rescue and, although seven of them were killed by Turkish fire, managed to drag him away to safety. Realizing that the train was far too heavily defended by Jemal's guards to permit their small band to take a chance on rushing it, Lawrence and Ali decided to retire from the scene of the wreckage carrying with the their wounded, including Fahad, who had been hit by bullet in the face.

❖   ❖   ❖

Back among the haunted ruins of Azrak Lawrence hesitated to return to Allenby and confess his failure face to face. In any case, he told himself, the rain had set in steadily and the British offensive would be bogged down; therefore if there was to be no action on any front, he would be best employed in staying at Azrak with Ali and spreading the message of the Arab Revolt among the tribes. In fact he was wrong and his miscalculations came perilously near to wrecking his influence with Allenby. For at that very moment the British Commander-in-Chief was carrying out a brilliant move which broke the Turkish front and opened the road to Jerusalem. Having with a feint attack deceived the enemy into thinking he was concentrating on Gaza at the western end of the line, he made his main thrust at the weak point in the Turkish defences near Beersheba to the east. The enemy, taken by surprise, broke under the attack and the British cavalry poured through the break into the hills of Judaea. Newcombe had covered himself in glory in this action, setting up a road block between Jerusalem and Beersheba and preventing enemy reinforcements being rushed up to plug the gap. With a handful of men he held this position for two days against furious Turkish attacks until he was taken prisoner when his ammunition ran out.

Lawrence was, of course, unaware of all this as he sat at Azrak receiving daily calls from the local Bedouin sheikhs and Druse chieftains who looked in from the deserts and mountains of Syria to enquire about the Arab Revolt. For a while he was content with the rôle of sedentary propagandist. After the hectic activity and constant strain of the past few weeks he found this new life soothing and restful; and he enjoyed greatly the company of Ali, whose physical perfection and grace combined with his wild strength of personality and a deep indestructible pride in his tribal heritage to make him a more than ordinarily attractive companion. Lawrence described their association as a "David and Jonathan" relationship.

But after a couple of weeks conscience began to prick and boredom set in. Lawrence had had time enough to realize that probably Allenby had been right in asking for a general uprising around Deraa. His daily contacts with the Syrian sheikhs had reconfirmed that they were ready for anything if the British were on the march. Also he had just gained an important recruit in Talal el Hareidhin, Sheikh of Tafas, a few miles to the north of Deraa. Talal was a well-known outlaw with a price on his head who had, so legend ran, killed twenty-three Turks with his own hand and he knew the country as none other. It was time for Lawrence to reconnoitre the Deraa district and lay plans for Allenby's advance and this was the man to act as his guide.

16

Lawrence and Talal set out together to scout the Deraa district. After several days spent circling the town and visiting the outlying villages, Lawrence decided to enter Deraa itself. Talal being too well-known to accompany him with any safety within the town limits, he went alone. He had hardly gone a few hundred yards when he was challenged by a Turkish sergeant and accused of being a deserter from the Ottoman army. Lawrence tried to bluff it out, saying he was a Circassian and Circassians were exempt from military service. But the sergeant merely retorted, "Nahi Bey wants you, come with me."

Inside the guard-room the sergeant quickly made it clear what the Bey wanted him for. If Lawrence fulfilled his pleasure, he would probably be let go; if not, he would be drafted for training at a Turkish infantry depot. According to Lawrence's own account he was marched to the governor's house and taken straight to the Bey's bedroom. Here he was told to sit on the floor. The Bey dismissed the guard, seized hold of his prisoner and pulled him onto the bed. Lawrence twisted out of the Turk's sweaty grasp and retreated towards the door. The Bey then tried cajolery, saying how white and fresh Lawrence looked to him and how he would be made an orderly with good pay if he would submit to making love. When Lawrence still resisted, Nahi Bey clapped his hands for the guard to come and hold his prisoner while he stripped him of his clothes and started to paw and fondle his flesh. Revolted by these attentions Lawrence did the only thing he could do with his arms held tight behind his back; and in the next moment the Bey was writhing in agony on the bed clutching his groin where Lawrence had hit him with a sudden jerk of his knee. In a frenzy of rage the Turk rushed at his prisoner and beat him across the face with his slipper, then bit him in the neck and finally lacerated his flesh with a bayonet that he grabbed from one of the guards. Dipping his pudgy finger in the blood and smearing it over Lawrence's stomach, he offered his victim one last chance to obey and, when Lawrence still mutely showed defiance, ordered the guard to take him out and teach him everything.

Held down by four soldiers, Lawrence was then flogged until he fainted. On coming to, he was flogged again and sodomized by each of his tormentors in turn. But, when he was dragged back to the Bey, he was mercifully rejected "as a thing too torn and bloody for his bed" and the young corporal who had whipped him had to stay and play substitute. Throughout this excruciating and degrading torture Lawrence's greatest fear was that he might give himself away by shouting out in English. At first he had bitten his lips raw to keep from making any sound; but when the pain had become too great he willed himself to groan only in Arabic until, as he put it, "before the end a merciful sickness choked my utterance."

When it was over he was escorted to an empty room, next to which was a dispensary where he found a suit of shoddy clothes. There he waited until dawn and then painfully and slowly put the suit on, climbed out of the window and slipped away down the deserted street.

On a first reading one is tempted to conclude that of all the extraordinary adventures and feats of endurance recorded by Lawrence in the *Seven Pillars of Wisdom* this account of what happened to him in Deraa is the only one that does not ring true. That he had trained his body, by such practices as scourging himself, to endure torture is a known fact; that he could stand more physical pain, weariness and sickness than the toughest of mortals is well established —yet it still seems incredible that, after such terrible punishment, he could within a few hours have pulled himself together sufficiently to escape from the town and return to his friends. Moreover, his own account relates that he not only returned post-haste to Azrak but on the very next day mounted his camel and rode three hundred miles back to Akaba covering the journey in less than seventy hours, a feat remarkable enough for a thoroughly fit man but scarcely credible for someone who had just been all but flogged to death.

What, then, is the truth about the Deraa incident? Was it as he wrote it, or was Lawrence concealing the real facts behind a piece of horror fiction? Not one of Lawrence's several biographers has given a satisfactory answer. Lowell Thomas, B. H. Liddell Hart, Robert Graves and J. B. Villars have all published Lawrence's own version without question. Richard Aldington disbelieves the story, along with everything else in the *Seven Pillars of Wisdom* that shows Lawrence in a heroic light. He claims that Lawrence did not in fact resist the Bey's homosexual advances and asserts that he admitted as much in a letter to Mrs. George Bernard Shaw. But Aldington is as usual misleading his readers for this letter makes it perfectly clear that Lawrence had first resisted and only to save himself *further* torture eventually gave in.

Another theory, advanced by Terence Rattigan in a stageplay based on the life of Lawrence, is that he was a suppressed homosexual and that the Turks knew this. From this premise the theory suggests that the Turks—or more precisely the governor of Deraa —decided that the way to destroy Lawrence, and, through destroying him, the Arab Revolt, was to break down his resistance and force him to submit to, and enjoy, a homosexual experience. Thus, when Lawrence obligingly stepped into the trap, the Bey proceeded with his plan and, having broken his victim's will, released him to return to his Arab friends. Though the Turkish soldiery were opposed to letting him go, and with him the hope of a share in the ten or twenty thousand pounds reward offered for his capture, the Bey pointed out to them that as a captive he would become a martyr and a hostage whom the Arabs would redouble their efforts to set free, whereas if released as a man morally and physically broken he would no longer have the power or the will to lead the Arabs in revolt.

Not only must this version be untrue; but it does not even make credible fiction. Whether or not Lawrence ever had a homosexual leaning or experience, there is no evidence to show that the Turks at Deraa knew who he was. Nor is there any reason to suppose that they saw through his pretence of being a Circassian—a perfectly possible deception since Circassians, being of European stock, are often fair-skinned and blue-eyed. Besides, it cannot be seriously suggested that, had the Bey guessed his real identity, he would have dared to release him, even supposing he had been un-Turkish enough to prefer playing the amateur psychiatrist to collecting the reward for his capture. Had he been found out—and, according to the theory, his soldiers also knew who their prisoner was— the Bey would have been instantly reported and in all probability hanged for treason.

In fact none of these versions carries conviction and the story of Deraa has remained a mystery. There is probably a very simple reason for this— the fact that in all his life Lawrence never told a living soul what really happened and died with the secret still intact. In a final chapter of this book an attempt is made to fathom these hidden depths where beyond doubt lies the principal key to what he did after the war and the desert campaign were over. For the moment suffice it to say that, whatever form the terrible experience he had undergone may have taken, it formed a spiritual turning-point in his life and he was changed thereafter into something altogether harder and less gentle in his treatment of himself and those about him.

❖ ❖ ❖

Back in Azrak, Lawrence quickly decided to stay no longer. Bidding a sad farewell to Ali and accompanied by only one member of his bodyguard, he set out to ride back to Akaba. It was a mad march. Rain, sleet and snow beat against them, tearing their faces and numbing their hands. Lawrence was suffering from fever and every lurch and stride of his camel was agony. Yet it was his companion who tired first, though the young man was among the most vigorous and energetic of his followers. Ignoring all pleas for a rest Lawrence pressed on.

> I found myself [he says] dividing into parts. There was one which went on riding wisely, sparing or helping every pace of the wearied camel. Another hovering above and to the right bent down curiously, and asked what the flesh was doing. The flesh gave no answer, for indeed it was conscious only of a ruling impulse to keep on and on; but a third garrulous one talked and wondered, critical of the body's self-inflicted labour, and contemptuous of the reason for effort.

That the second was the dominant part there can be no doubt. Forcing himself far beyond the limits of ordinary endurance, Lawrence seemed to delight in anticipating the moment when his mind and body would finally collapse under the strain. He knew that this point was not far off, but equally he was determined to reach Akaba before the inevitable collapse. This he did, riding into the town, down the dried-up wadi that once guided the Jordan river into the Red Sea, on the afternoon of the third day out from Azrak.

At Akaba Joyce gave him the news of Allenby's

successes and five days later, during which he never
spoke a single word, he was sent for by the Commander-in-Chief to report on his activities. As he
entered Allenby's office, he presented an almost
tragically different picture to the bumptious, bouncing
victor of Akaba; but fortunately for him, Allenby
was too busy directing the final moves in the capture
of Jerusalem to be concerned with Lawrence's sufferings, of which in any case he probably knew nothing. Also he was too wise a judge of men to con-
demn him for the Yarmuk failure. So, instead of re-
criminating or dismissing his young subordinate—as
Lawrence might have expected—Allenby told him to
stay around and, when Jerusalem fell on 9th December, invited him to join in the ceremonial entry of
the British forces into the golden city, although—as
Lawrence rather ruefully remarked—"I had done
nothing for the success."

17

Back at headquarters after the celebrations and cere-
monies of Jerusalem, Lawrence discussed plans with
Allenby and his staff. Much to his relief, he discovered that the Commander-in-Chief had not lost
faith in the Arab movement. On the contrary: he was
full of ideas as to how Feisal could help his further
advance. It was decided that the Arabs should move
up to the Dead Sea as soon as possible and stop the
passage of Turkish food transports to Jericho, which
was to be the objective of Allenby's next offensive in
February. They were then to advance to the northern
end of the Dead Sea and to link up with the British
armies at the Jordan river in March. Feisal was already
planning to move on Tafileh near the south-eastern
corner of the Dead Sea, so it was clear that their
plans would conveniently converge.

After a week's leave in Cairo, Lawrence returned
to Akaba to find the place once more throbbing with
activity. Captain Pisani, the commander of the small
French contingent at Akaba, had got some new
French mountain guns. New rifles, machine-guns and
automatic weapons had arrived in great numbers.
Talbot, Rolls-Royce and Ford armoured cars and
troop-carriers were being unloaded; and the three
thousand regular troops of Feisal's army were being
drilled and trained into an effective fighting unit by
Jaafar and Nuri es Said, a former Arab officer of the
Turkish army who later became Prime Minister of
Iraq and was murdered in the revolution of 1958.
Maulud, in spite of the handicap of intense cold,

had virtually driven the Turks from Aba el Lissan and was threatening Maan. The Hejaz railway was of course also under constant attack by Arab demolition parties.

Lawrence and Joyce decided to try out the new armoured cars in a raid on Mudauwra to fill in time while the expeditionary force was being prepared for the march to the Dead Sea. The car crews were mostly English and included appropriately enough a man called Rolls, who has himself written an account of the exploits he shared with Lawrence in these armoured cars. He is not alone in testifying to Lawrence's mania for speed, whether it was on a racing camel, a motor bicycle or in a car or a speedboat. Speed was his drug, as Ronald Storrs put it, and, like many another addict, he died of an overdose in the end. Racing across the smooth mud flats between Guweira and Mudauwra at sixty to seventy miles an hour, he and his men rejoiced at this wonderful new freedom and speed of movement. Instead of mining a train they decided to shoot up a couple of enemy blockhouses to see how the cars could be manoeuvred in this kind of open attack. Although the raid itself accomplished little except to give the Turks a nasty fright, it proved one highly important thing—that with the speed and protection of armoured cars they could operate against the railway and its guard-posts at will.

There was, however, another lesson which Lawrence had learned twelve months before in the Hejaz fighting but which he still seemed unable to get his British superiors to accept—that the Bedouin could only perform effectively in guerilla-type operations and were no good at European-style warfare. Allenby came to accept this in the end but at the beginning of 1918 he was still not convinced. Though a great believer in mobility, he could not altogether divorce himself from the concept of moving in formation and he had sent General Dawnay to Akaba to instil these ideas into the Emir's army.

Unable to prevent this either by representations to headquarters or by enlisting the support of the regular Arab officers who, being Turkish-trained, were themselves addicted to more regular standards, Lawrence reacted by enlarging his bodyguard to a strength of some ninety men, all of them mercenaries or former bandits trained by hard experience to desert fighting and of fearless courage and absolute loyalty. With a band of this strength and determination he could operate independently whenever he wished. Also he admitted that he felt the need of this much protection, the Turks having just raised the price for his capture to twenty thousand pounds alive or ten thousand dead. The British officers at Akaba disapprovingly called these men cutthroats, "but they only cut throats to my order," Lawrence replied. The Arabs, on the other hand, were full of admiration. Always ready to enthuse over a good piece of stage management, they marvelled at this further demonstration of showmanship. A leader who could equip himself with such an escort, armed with modern submachine guns, dressed in the finest robes and riding the fastest camels, must be a great leader indeed. They did not stop to think that the money these men were being paid came, not from Lawrence, but out of the gold which Feisal had been given by the British, the arms were "borrowed" by Lawrence from British ordnance, the camels were Feisal's property and the clothes probably stolen in desert raids on the tribal tents of their own neighbours.

❖   ❖   ❖

About the middle of January all was set for the capture of Tafileh, the gateway to the Dead Sea. The plan was to attack from three sides, east, south and west. The eastern group was under the command of Sherif Nasir with Nuri es Said in charge of the guns. They approached via Jurf, a station on the Hejaz railway, which once taken would prevent Turkish reinforcements rushing either from Maan in the south or Amman in the north to interfere with the main attack on Tafileh. Jurf fell easily to Nuri's guns and Nasir, now joined by Auda, marched on to Tafileh. When they got there a day before the other groups coming up from the south, they found the village defended by a mere hundred and eighty Turks and some armed villagers. The villagers were in a state of feud with a neighbouring clan which had declared for Feisal and opened fire as Nasir's force advanced, whereupon Auda, enraged at their audacity—for he thought himself their secular chieftain—galloped to the village entrance and boomed at the astonished inmates. "Dogs, do you not know Auda?" It was enough both for the villagers and for the Turks. Within an hour Nasir was drinking tea with the Turkish governor in the not altogether unhappy rôle of the Sherif's guest and prisoner.

That night the Emir Zeid, Hussein's youngest son, whom Feisal had put in command of the advance to the Dead Sea, arrived in Tafileh with Jaafar and Lawrence. This caused an awkward situation, for it transpired that the father of two young members of Zeid's retinue had been killed by Auda's son. When they started muttering about revenge, the old man scoffed and spat at them that they resembled a couple of tomtits threatening a hawk and said that he would whip them in the village market place if they persisted in such talk. Zeid, taking the line of least resistance, packed Auda and his warriors off back to the desert—a weakening of his strength that was to prove almost fatal.

Zeid was now left to hold Tafileh with a hundred camel men, Lawrence's bodyguard and a detachment of Egyptian and French Moroccan machine-gunners. Nuri es Said's artillery had not been able to cross the snow-bound passes of the Moab mountains and had stayed behind to hold Jurf with Sherif Nasir. It It was a dangerously small garrison if the Turks should try to retake Tafileh with any strength but there was nothing for it but to dig in and hope that they would remain unmolested until the weather improved and reinforcements could reach them.

This was not to be. On 25th January, only nine days after its capture, the Turks came back to Tafileh and counter-attacked with three battalions of infantry, nine hundred strong, a hundred cavalry, two mountain guns and twenty-seven machine-guns. Taken completely by surprise, the Arabs panicked, the village was thrown into complete confusion and most of the villagers, fearing Turkish reprisals for having surrendered without a shot to Auda and Nasir, fled into the hills. Zeid and Jaafar proposed to withdraw from the village and defend themselves from a ravine to the south of the village, a notion which Lawrence opposed as doubly unsound, because the ravine was not a good defensive position and by quitting Tafileh they would throw away those stout-hearted villagers who had stayed and would be useful additional defenders. But Zeid was in command and insisted on giving the order to withdraw.

It did not take him long to realize the error of his decision and, with only a few minutes left before the Turkish attack fell upon them, he abdicated his command. Lawrence immediately set about defending the village, posting his few troops and armed villagers in stepped formations on the slopes of a series of ridges in front of Tafileh, while one of his bodyguards—Abdulla, nicknamed the Robber—went ahead to draw the enemy fire with a couple of Hotchkiss machine-guns. The Turks opened up with their mountain guns while these manoeuvres were taking place and plastered the ridge with shells and shrapnel. Then, as the enemy advanced, the Arabs retired gradually from one ridge to another, blunting the attack and breaking its momentum as they withdrew. Meanwhile, reinforcements arrived for the defenders in the form of two hundred armed villagers and a hundred tribesmen from a nearby camp. This was exactly what Lawrence needed. His plan had been to lure the Turks progressively onto the ridges and then attack their flanks with every gun he had. With these reinforcements he would now have enough men for a three-sided attack and would not have to weaken the final ridge before Tafileh in order to spring his trap.

Silently the tribesmen crept up to the Turkish machine-guns and, opening fire at three hundred yards' range, wiped out every gun team. Then on the other flank a small group of mounted Arabs charged the Turkish infantry and cut them to pieces. Seeing this slaughter of their comrades on the left and right flanks, the Turks in the centre broke and ran in wild disorder, hotly pursued by the victorious Arabs and the Armenian villagers whose drawn knives made short work of the slower fugitives. When the firing had ceased the Arabs counted their captures, which included every gun the Turks had brought with them, two hundred horses and mules and two hundred and fifty prisoners. Only fifty of the eleven hundred Turks got back to their base alive; of the rest, those who were not killed in the action either died of exposure from being left wounded in the snow or were cut down as they tried to escape.

It had been a remarkable battle and a tremendous triumph for Lawrence's leadership and courage. But he himself dismissed it, somewhat typically, with disparaging phrases about its "orthodoxy." His own report to headquarters "was mainly written for effect, full of quaint similes and mock simplicities; and made them think me a modest amateur, doing his best after the great models; not a clown, leering after them. . . . Like the battle it was nearly-proof parody of regulation use. Headquarters loved it, and innocently, to crown the jest, offered me a decoration on the strength of it. We should have more bright breasts in the Army, if each man was able without witnesses to write out his own despatch."

A typical piece of Lawrenciana this—impish, vain, but with a strong overtone of self-criticism. From his own account he was clearly angry and bitter at being trapped into such an engagement, which did not square with his ideas of how to conduct the Arab campaign—his principle of containment without combat. Apart from the unplanned action at Aba el Lissan, Tafileh was the only pitched battle that he ever fought, and this could well be a reason why he disparaged it so severely. In his comment upon the casualties suffered by the Arabs he remarked bitterly, "It was one-sixth of our force gone on a verbal triumph, for the destruction of this thousand poor Turks would not affect the issue of the war. . . . (Tafileh's) sole profit lay, then, in its lesson to myself."

Yet, however he may have resented his trumph because expediency had driven him to use the methods of the training manuals to bring it off, its results enabled Lawrence and his Arabs to operate without further opposition in bringing to a standstill the Turkish supply traffic across the Dead Sea to their armies at Jericho.

18

On 28th January 1918, two weeks earlier than the deadline set by Allenby, Lawrence stopped the Turkish Dead Sea traffic with a raid of the utmost daring. With some seventy horsemen he rode through the night to Kerak, the lake port which the Turks used to ferry their wheat and barley from the granaries of the fertile plains of this area. Information had reached him that a flotilla of Turkish food lighters was making ready to depart the following day for the Jericho sector, under the escort of an armed motor launch. As a grey dawn broke across the sky, the Arabs charged down to the seashore and into the water before the slumbering unsuspecting crews had time to pull themselves together. Taken by surprise the Turks scarcely resisted and in a few moments the whole operation was completed. The storage huts in the port were burned, the stores looted and the lighters taken out to sea and scuttled. Without a casualty of their own and with sixty Turkish prisoners the Arabs returned with much laughter and self-congratulation to the base at Tafileh, having probably made history by providing the only case on record of a naval engagement being won by cavalry!

Lawrence had fulfilled the first two of the three assignments upon which he and Allenby had agreed. There remained the third task—linking up with the British armies at the Jordan river north of the Dead Sea by March. But as February arrived the prospects of meeting this deadline began to look bleak. The weather had worsened considerably and to venture forth with the necessary camel force in thick snow through the mountains of Moab which lay between Tafileh and the north would have been madness. If the camels did not die of exposure, they would present an easy target to a few Turkish horsemen as they plunged and slithered clumsily up and down the icy mountain defiles.

At the same time, to stay in Tafileh held few attractions or compensations. At five thousand feet above sea level the cold was intense, fuel was scarce and living conditions cruel. "We were penned in verminous houses of cold stone; lacking fuel, lacking food; storm bound in streets like sewers, amid blizzards of sleet and an icy wind . . . the fleas on the stone floor sang together nightly, for praise of the new meats given them. We were twenty-eight in the two tiny rooms which reeked with the sour smell of our crowd." Lawrence, indulging his love of the classics, sought consolation in reading *Morte d' Arthur;* but the Arabs, having no such digressions, fell to quarrelling among themselves. Two of his bodyguard started a fight with daggers and on being separated by the others were flogged for the offence of breaking faith with the pledge of *rafiq*.

Meanwhile Zeid was running short of money. Most of the gold which was to be spent in organizing the march to the Jordan had been distributed in rewards for service at the battle of Tafileh. Lawrence jumped at the excuse to get away from these verminous conditions and to go to collect more supplies. It was early in February and blowing a blizzard when he set off to the south. The journey was rough, the camels and their riders being quite unused to travelling in such conditions. But Lawrence, as usual, drove himself, his men and his beasts to the very limit of endurance and on the afternoon of the second day they arrived, "filthy and miserable, stringy like shaven cats," at Guweira, now the headquarters of the British armoured car unit and the liaison staff with Feisal. There he found Dawnay and Joyce plunged in

gloom. Feisal had tried to capture Mudauwra a fortnight earlier with a mixed force of tribesmen and four
companies of Arab regulars supported by Pisani's
French guns. He had suffered a humiliating defeat.
The tribesmen, typically, had abandoned the struggle
when the first attack failed to dislodge the Turks
and Pisani had come very near to losing his guns in
the withdrawal. Lawrence received the news phil-
osophically, no doubt reflecting with a certain *schad-
enfreude* that it would teach Feisal to follow his advice
in future and discourage the Turkish-trained Arab
officers and their British colleagues in their predilec-
tion for text-book warfare.

After a brief conference with Feisal, Lawrence set
off to return to Tafileh with thirty thousand pounds
worth of gold packed in his saddle-bags. The return
journey was, if anything, worse than the ride to Guweira, with sleet and snow and biting winds half
strangling him and his two Ateiba companions as
they climbed onto the long spine of mountains that
stretch to the southern tip of the Dead Sea. Somewhere above Aba el Lissan he came across a group of
Maulud's men living in shallow dug-outs in the hill-
side, a mountain guardpost keeping watch on Turkish movements along the Hejaz railway. With no fuel
except some wet scrub, and clad in British summer-
weight khaki uniforms, they had lost more than half
of their number from cold and exposure. Yet still
they kept watch and kept harrying any Turkish caravans that came within range of their deadly rifle-
fire.

Lawrence was enormously impressed by their courage. "We owed much to them," he says, "and more
to Maulud, whose fortitude stiffened them in their
duty . . . with [his] sturdy sense of Arab honour
and nationality . . . a strong creed which enabled
him to endure cheerfully three winter months in front
of Maan and to share out enough spirit among five
hundred ordinary men to keep them stout-heart-
edly about him." Determined to be no less stout-

hearted himself, he forced his frozen body and his over-burdened camels on across the mountains. Once he nearly drowned in a half-frozen stream. Then his camel collapsed in a snow-bound pass and only after much coaxing and tugging was finally persuaded to rise and continue the journey back to Tafileh. Here Lawrence handed over his treasure to Zeid amid much rejoicing from the Emir's men who had been without pay as well as without comforts for several weeks.

Instructing the young Emir, once the troops had been paid, to keep the balance of the gold for future operations, Lawrence laid his exhausted body down to rest. As he collapsed on the floor a voice spoke to him in English. "Would you like my blanket? You look frozen stiff." The speaker was Lieutenant Kirk-bride, then an officer of the Royal Engineers and one day to become British Ambassador in Jordan, who had been sent by G.H.Q. to examine the pos-sibilities of building a motor road from Beersheba through the mountain passes to Tafileh, a project which he had satisfied himself was quite impractic-able. "I think you'll agree with my findings after what you've just been through," he told Lawrence, laughing as he collected a blanket from each of the protesting group of Arabs that shared the hovel with the two Englishmen. "Indeed," came the reply, "you'd better join up with me instead of going on these wild-goose chases for headquarters." Kirkbride, a lean twenty-year-old, beamed at the invitation. Fluent in Arabic and trained in intelligence and dem-olition work, as well as being young and enthusi-astic, Lawrence felt that he would make the perfect assistant. "I'll ask for you to be transferred, then." The two shook hands and so began a partnership that was to last until Damascus and to save Lawrence's life on more than one occasion.

The following day Lawrence went off with Kirk-bride and his bodyguard to reconnoitre the route to the Jordan. The thaw had just begun and it might still be possible to keep his appointed rendezvous with Allenby in the month of March, a little over a fortnight ahead. The reconnaissance proved most satisfactory. "Each step of our road to join the British was possible; most of them easy," and he returned to Zeid in high spirits. But, as he outlined his plan of march, the Emir interrupted him to say that it would require a great deal more money to finance the advance.

"Not at all," Lawrence retorted, "the funds in hand will cover it and more."

Zeid shifted nervously in his seat and Lawrence, growing suspicious, pressed him to say how much he had left of the gold that had come from Guweira. Zeid, looking down at the floor, said shamefacedly, "It is all gone; I have spent it all in recompensing the Sheikh of Tafileh, the villagers and the tribesmen."

"But you know that the custom is only to pay the tribesmen when they are on active service, not when they are resting up in winter quarters," Lawrence protested, aghast at this prodigality.

"Even so, I paid them," replied Zeid coldly, like a guilty child caught in the act of mischief.

This was the end of any hope that the Arabs might join hands with Allenby in March. It would be impossible to mount the operation without money and it would be asking too much to expect headquarters to ante up the extravagances of Zeid. While Lawrence was pondering this dilemma and finding no solution, Joyce arrived unexpectedly from Guweira. He offered to return to Feisal and ask for his help, but Zeid was not enthusiastic and Lawrence had made up his mind to return to headquarters and ask for another assignment.

❖ ❖ ❖

How seriously this decision to abdicate should be taken is difficult to say. There is no doubt that Lawrence was extremely fed up with Zeid, who had been weak, stubborn and foolish from the moment he assumed command of the Dead Sea operations. He wanted no further responsibility for the young Emir's follies. But that Lawrence wanted no further part in the Arab Revolt is hardly credible at this stage. True, he told Allenby at his headquarters near Beersheba that he had had enough of responsibility and wanted a job where he would be given orders. "I complained that since landing in Arabia I had had options and requests but never an order; that I was tired to death of free will." To himself he added that "these worries would have taken their due petty place . . . but for the rankling fraudulence which had to be my mind's habit: that pretence to lead the national uprising of another race, the daily posturing in alien dress, preaching in alien speech; with behind it a sense that the 'promises' on which the Arabs worked were worth what their armed strength would be when the moment of fulfilment came." Perhaps Zeid's ineffectiveness—and Feisal's apparent unwisdom when left to his own devices—had already persuaded him that the Arabs would never have the strength to enforce the fulfilment of the Allies' promises. Was this, then, the moment when his visions of power and glory started to fade? Somehow this seems doubtful. Certainly his experiences at Tafileh, the shocking waste of life in the battle and the waste of money that followed, preyed on his mind and made him wonder at times which was the greater fraud—the Arab Revolt or the British pledges that inspired it. But, if at this stage he had really foreseen the tragedy that was to prove his Arab allies unequal to the forces ranged against them, Lawrence would hardly have been persuaded as easily as he himself recorded to return to Feisal and organize fresh plans for the advance of the Arab armies.

More likely he was jerked out of his pessimism by the good news and the ambitious plans which greeted him at headquarters. Jericho had just fallen and Allenby was poised for the final thrust into Syria. General Jan Smuts had come from the Imperial War Cabinet in London to urge that Turkey be put out of the war as soon as possible so as to release troops for the still hard-pressed Western front in France and Flanders. Allenby told Lawrence that he looked to his eastern—Arab—flank to help in this last burst to Damascus and that this was no time to weaken the effectiveness of the Arab army by withdrawing its principal guide and mentor.

This, it appears, was enough for Lawrence. He had made his explanations and apologies and by tendering his resignation had offered himself as sacrifice. He could now return to galvanize Feisal into the final thrust that could, indeed must, get the Arab armies to Damascus before anyone else. On 4th March 1918 he was back at Akaba.

19

The new plan of action decided by Allenby was to launch an attack across the Jordan from Jericho on 5th May, to split the Turkish armies defending the line between Jaffa and the north of the Dead Sea, to occupy Salt—some twenty miles west of Amman— and, in preparation for a later push, to destroy the railway south of Amman. The Arab armies' part in these operations was to capture Maan and its garrison and to join up with the British north of Jericho.

For this purpose Lawrence was the bearer of the happy news to Feisal that he would receive three hundred thousand pounds in gold to buy whatever local and tribal support was necessary, seven hundred pack camels, plus artillery and machine-guns. The rejoicing that greeted this handsome offer from Allenby was not even damped by the almost simultaneous news that Zeid had lost Tafileh to a Turkish counter-attack. Feisal expressed a passing fear that its recapture might damage his reputation and Lawrence seized upon the disappointment to read the Emir a severe lecture on the incompetence of his young brother and the bitter waste of a valuable advance for which he had been responsible. Then both of them turned without further recrimination to future business.

With Joyce and Jaafer they made their dispositions for the capture of Maan. Jaafar and Nuri es Said would attack with the Arab regulars; Dawnay and Joyce would cut the Hejaz railway at Mudauwra— but permanently this time to isolate the Turks in Medina; and Lawrence was to raise the Beni Sakhr

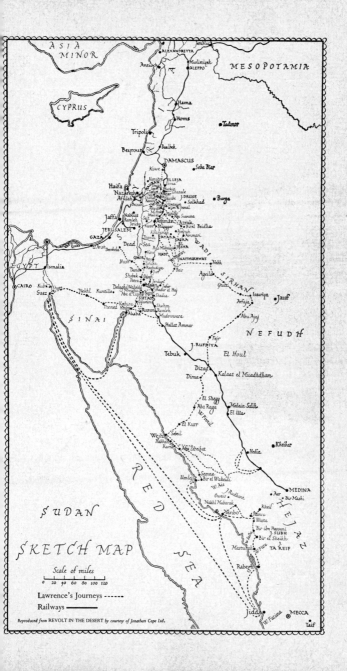

SKETCH MAP

Scale of miles
0 20 40 60 80 100 120

Lawrence's Journeys -----
Railways _____

Reproduced from REVOLT IN THE DESERT by courtesy of Jonathan Cape Ltd.

Lawrence — In India with the
R.A.F. as Aircraftman T. E. Shaw

Emir Feisal

Feisal's army advancing on Wejh, January 1917

Wells at Wejh

Rolls-Royce tender at Akaba. Colonel Joyce in the front seat

Captain T. E. Lawrence

Field-Marshal Viscount Allenby
and Emir Feisal

Emir Abdulla with Sherif Ali
ibn el Hussein

The Yarmuk River bridge, which survived all Lawrence's efforts to destroy it

"El Aurens," Akaba, 1917

The triumphal entry into Akaba,
July 1917

The Versailles Conference: Emir Feisal's delegation with Nuri es
Said and Lawrence flanking Feisal, and Captain Pisani in the centre

Auda abu Tayi (2nd from right) and Howeitat chiefs

Aircraftman T. E. Shaw

Lawrence on his motor-bike with George Brough, its manufacturer

The library of Lawrence's cottage at Clouds Hill, Dorset

tribe in the Amman area directly news came of the capture of Salt and then to attack the retreating Turks from behind. The plan for the Maan operation was to post the Arab army across the railway to the north, cut the town off from any hope of reinforcement or supply, and draw the enemy into the open. But, when Maulud and the regular Arab officers got to hear of this, they opposed it violently. Maulud insisted heatedly upon a direct assault. The argument raged over several days but in the end Feisal took the line of least resistance and allowed Maulud to have his way, the issue having become a matter of face and honour for the old warrior and his lieutenants.

With grave misgivings as to the wisdom of this decision and the weakness which Feisal had shown, Lawrence rode off at the beginning of April to set up his base at Atara, southeast of Amman and the centre of the Beni Sakhr country, where Mifleh and Fahad were awaiting him. On the way he received word that Daud, one of the two original members of his bodyguard, had died of cold at Azrak, where he had stayed behind with Sheikh Ali after the Deraa incident. Lawrence was deeply affected by this tragedy, not least because the news plunged Farraj, Daud's faithful lover and companion, into inconsolable misery, driving out the imp that was in him and had provided so much merriment on so many weary miles of march since the long trek to Akaba. "The others offered themselves to comfort him, but instead he wandered restlessly, grey and silent, very much alone." It was clear that life held no further joy for the wretched Farraj and that it was only a question of time before he would find an opportunity to end it.

The occasion arose a few weeks later. After their arrival at Atara, word came that the British had captured not only Salt but Amman as well. Lawrence gave the order to close on the retreating enemy. But no sooner had he started than a further message arrived to say that the Turks had retaken both towns and were chasing Allenby's army down the Jordan valley. Jemal Pasha would probably be back in Jerusalem in a few days. Meanwhile, to make the Arabs' flesh creep even more, there were rumours of wholesale hangings in Salt of those Arabs who had welcomed the British advance. Apparently undaunted by his experience at Deraa, Lawrence again decided to go and investigate for himself. Entering Amman with Farraj, disguised as two village women, he discovered soon enough that the Turks were in control of the town, if not of their sexual desires. For a moment later the two were sprinting down the street pursued by some Turkish soldiers out for a night's frivolity who took them for a couple of nice young prostitutes.

There being evidently no British advance to link up with and no Turkish retreat to harass and with the local Bedouins severely shaken by the tales of Turkish reprisals, Lawrence had no alternative but to withdraw to Feisal's headquarters and wait for Allenby to strike again. On the journey south he and his bodyguard ran into a patrol of eight Turks on the railway. The Arabs wanted to attack but Lawrence thought it better not to waste bullets on so small a group. Then suddenly, as he was speaking, Farraj galloped forward heedless of his master's words. The rest joined in but Farraj was too far out in front, offering an easy target to the Turkish rifles. The first shot went right through him, smashing his spine and tearing a wide gash in his stomach, which was pouring forth a steady stream of blood by the time his companions reached him. As they were wondering whether and how he might be saved, the alarm was given that a patrol of fifty Turks was approaching down the railway line. Lawrence decided in a flash that he must give Farraj the *coup de grâce*—anything rather than let him fall into Turkish hands and suffer the torture and mutilations which the enemy meted out to the Arabs they caught in combat. The Turks were known to burn alive wounded captives and it had been agreed between him and his men that they would finish one another off, if badly injured. Lawrence described most movingly the last moments of Farraj.

> I knelt down beside him, holding my pistol near the ground by his head, so that he should not see my purpose; but he must have guessed it, for he opened his eyes, and clutched me with his harsh scaly hand, the tiny hand of these unripe Nejd fellows. I waited a moment, and he said, "Daud will be angry with you," the old smile coming back so strangely to this grey shrinking face. I replied, "Salute him from me." He returned the formal answer, "God will give you peace," and at last wearily closed his eyes.

At Feisal's headquarters near Maan Lawrence found that Allenby had indeed failed to hold Salt and that the Arabs, as he expected, had not been able to take Maan. Nuri's artillery fire was proving inadequate to storm the town; Maulud had been wounded; and Auda was quarrelling with everybody, including Feisal and Nuri, whom he blamed for insisting on tactics which were quite unsuitable for tribesmen— an accusation to which Nuri retorted that the Howeitat had been quite useless. Nuri had led a storming party into the Maan railway station but when Pisani's guns ran out of shells he had been forced to retire. The only success had been the cutting of the railway beyond hope of early repair ten miles to the south of the town.

For good measure, Dawnay followed this up with an armoured car raid on Mudauwra, accompanied by Lawrence and two new English officers who had just joined—Hornby, a sapper and demolition expert, and Peake, who was later to found the Arab Legion of Transjordan. The operation was a success, the railway being broken beyond even the power of Fakhri Pasha to mend it again. But all that this rail cutting was doing was to bottle up the Turks in their strong-

holds—Medina, Maan and Amman—without helping
Feisal to advance along the right flank of the Allied
front. Once again Lawrence feared that the Arabs'
failure to keep to an agreed plan might lose them the
favour of the Commander-in-Chief. Once again, therefore, he dashed off to make his excuses and apologies
to Allenby. His arrival at headquarters in Jerusalem
was greeted by the news that the British were back in
Salt, thanks to the help of the Beni Sakhr sheikhs
who had come secretly to Jericho to offer their services in staging an uprising of twenty thousand tribesmen to coincide with the next British attack.

Lawrence could not believe his ears. It was bad
enough that the British should after all have kept to
the scheduled plan while the Arabs had fallen so painfully short; but that this should have been done in his
absence with the aid of the Arab tribesmen whom he
was supposed to raise was a double insult to his pride
and prestige. Also there was another unwelcome as-
pect to this affair. A British captain called Young
had just been appointed by Cairo to act as Lawrence's assistant liaison officer with the Sherifian
army. Young was a fluent Arabist and an orthodox
soldier, whom Lawrence had resented and distrusted
from his first arrival, suspecting him of being sent to
report on his superior's activities. Wishing to get rid
of him as soon as possible, Lawrence had sent Young
to hold a watching brief in the area between Maan
and Amman, the very area of the Beni Sakhr where, as
Allenby's staff officers had gleefully told Lawrence,
the British had raised the tribes to help them retake
Salt.

This was altogether too much for Lawrence's vanity
and it must be admitted that he was much relieved to
hear a few hours later that the attack had miscarried
and the British had been forced once more to withdraw, largely because the Beni Sakhr sheikhs had failed
to live up to their undertakings. Lawrence did not hes-
itate to rub into Allenby's staff that in future they
would be better advised to consult him before acting

on Arab promises which could not be honoured. Apart from this, a second British withdrawal gave him an alibi for the Arabs and "taught the British to be more patient with Feisal's difficulties." He was now able to argue that "Allenby's pause had stuck us with the siege of a superior force" at Maan.

All in all, there can be little doubt that Lawrence must have behaved at his exasperating worst on this visit to headquarters. Never exactly the darling of the staff, at least on other occasions he was arguing for a cause and seeking support for a campaign. His arguments and his tone were often arrogant and designed to assert his superior knowledge; yet he could then claim to be conducting almost singlehanded a remarkably courageous and successful operation. But on this occasion he behaved like a spoiled child making excuses for his own failures and gloating quite unworthily over those of his British comrades.

How Allenby tolerated this behaviour is a tribute to the patience and vast human understanding of that very great commander. He had enough to worry about at this time without having to endure this waspish critic as well. He had been enjoined by the Imperial War Cabinet to finish off the Turks as soon as possible; yet the War Office in London was at the same time stripping him of troops to strengthen the European front. The replacement of Indian troops from Mesopotamia which had been promised him in exchange had not arrived. Forced to postpone his offensive, all he could do until he was reinforced was to hold on and hope that the Turks would not counter-attack in strength. Then, on top of all these worries, Lawrence came to ask for concentrated air attacks on the Hejaz railway, on Maan and Amman to dislodge the Turks and force them into the open. Allenby called in General Salmond, who commanded the Air Force, and this was agreed. Lawrence then raised his bid, asking to be given the two thousand camels of the Imperial Camel Brigade in Sinai which was to be disbanded, save for one battalion under

Colonel Buxton. Allenby called in his Quartermaster General and in his presence asked Lawrence why he wanted these beasts. Without a moment's hesitation Lawrence boasted, "To put a thousand men in Deraa any day you please." Allenby smiled and, shaking his head at the Quartermaster, said, "Q, you lose."

It might almost be thought that for someone in Lawrence's position at that particular moment to be able to command such personal relations with his Commander-in-Chief and such unfailing support from him would require some special hypnotic powers. But in fact Allenby had complete faith in this unpredictable young officer, probably a greater faith than Lawrence had in himself towards the end of the campaign. In testifying to "his brilliance as a war leader," Allenby later wrote, "Lawrence was under my command, but, after acquainting him with my strategical plan, I gave him a free hand. His co-operation was marked by the utmost loyalty, and I never had anything but praise for his work, which indeed was valuable throughout the campaign."

Had Allenby not seen these qualities beneath the vain and insolent veneer, Lawrence would almost certainly have been finished after his first failure, for he had too many enemies at headquarters and in Cairo to get by without the personal support of the Commander-in-Chief. In retrospect he realized well enough the depth of his indebtedness, although in the heat of the moment he was probably more preoccupied with getting all he could of money and supplies out of headquarters and dashing off back to Feisal to announce his triumph and to prove his indispensability to the Emir's future plans.

20

The wildest rejoicing greeted Lawrence's return to Feisal's camp. The Emir gasped at the news of the two thousand camels. For a moment he was speechless and then, leaping to his feet and kissing Lawrence, clapped his hands for his slaves to summon Auda, Zaal, Fahad and the other sheikhly commanders of his army. When they were all assembled, Feisal told them that Allah had sent them the gift of unlimited mobility by which the Arabs would now march unchecked to triumph and freedom. Lawrence was warmly thanked and congratulated on his magnificent coup, after which the sheikhs, led of course by Auda, fell to boasting to one another of the wild deeds they would perform with this marvellous new strength added to their arms.

Lawrence hurried off to tell Joyce the good news. This was the supreme moment. The means of victory had been presented to him; at long last he held in his hand the key that would unlock the gates of Damascus. All the pain and humiliation of the past two years had been worthwhile now that he knew he could achieve the glorious end. The throne of Syria beckoned to its king and the kingmaker now stood ready to bring him in triumph to answer the call, borne forward irresistibly upon wave after wave of the laughing, singing throngs of his followers: and all this would be his doing, the result of his indispensable services to the Emir. Now he could be certain of the prizes which this grateful prince would lavish upon his friend and servant. To make doubly certain he had gone through the motions of suggesting to Feisal that the moment of victory would also mark the moment of his release. Feisal had protested, as Lawrence hoped and expected, that he "must remain with them always and not just till Damascus, as I had promised in Um Lejh." In truth, he would now be the power behind the throne of Arabia.

But the sunshine of this heroic moment was to pass as rapidly as it had come. Just as the dream seemed to glisten most brilliantly with hope and promise, the black shadows and sinister shapes of nightmare began to transform it. Within a month everything Lawrence had striven for started steadily to disintegrate, as the knowledge came to him that there was not going to be a free, united and independent Arabia, because the Arabs were too disunited and Feisal too weak to bring it to life. Up till this moment he had refused to be subdued by the most ominous signs. He had carried on in spite of his knowledge that the Allies were conspiring to make Arabia their vassal, believing—or forcing himself to believe—that the Arabs would show enough strength and unity to stand up for their rights and enforce the fulfilment of the British promises to Hussein, when the Turks had been driven out of their lands. He had been angry but never thwarted when the Arabs had let him and themselves down, blaming their failure on a shortage of men or guns or camels. But at the very time when these deficiencies were about to be made good permanently and the prospect of an early victory loomed near, he was to discover that the real deficiencies of the Sherifian armies lay in the heart of the Sherifian family and not in its material resources.

This tragic revelation came to Lawrence in the middle of June. Nasir, Auda and he had returned from a raid on the Hejaz railway designed to prevent the Turks relieving their beleaguered garrison in Maan with reinforcements which were reported to be massing at Amman. Although bombed by Turkish aircraft, they had done a thorough job, blowing up four miles of rail, three bridges and all the station buildings at Hesa, sixty miles from Maan, and another station further north. Lawrence explained to Feisal that this good work would mean that the Turks in the Amman sector would be immobilized for at least a month, possibly three, by which time the new camels would be fit for operations. Allenby's offensive had had to be put off until October because he would not have enough troops until then. If the Arabs were to attack independently in September when the camels would be ready, they would have every chance of capturing Damascus on their own.

Lawrence suggested to Feisal that Hussein be asked to transfer the regular units under Ali and Abdulla to his army to join in this independent Arab offensive. This would raise Feisal's regular forces to ten thousand, which could be divided into three parts —one to continue holding Maan besieged, the second to attack in the Deraa-Damascus sector and the third to follow up after making a junction with Allenby's armies at Jericho. The attack on the Deraa-Damascus sector would force the Turks to withdraw a division from Palestine and so help Allenby to back up the Arab attack. It would also mean that the Arabs would be entering Damascus just when the British began their own advance. Thus they could profit from British support without being prevented by it.

Feisal readily agreed to this plan and dispatched the necessary letters to his father in Mecca. Lawrence next asked Wingate, who had succeeded McMahon in Cairo, to add a letter of his own to the Grand Sherif making it plain that the British fully endorsed Feisal's request for regular reinforcements and that the old man would be ill-advised to refuse a demand backed by his British paymaster. This accomplished—although Lawrence records that the High Commissioner's letter could have been a lot stronger in tone—he went to G.H.Q. to inform Allenby. The Commander-in-Chief smiled and said that he was just too late. The replacements from India were now arriving and three days before Lawrence turned up he had advanced the date of his final offensive to September. The Arab armies would not therefore be attacking independently but alongside their British allies.

Lawrence took this well enough, although he must have been bitterly disappointed that the Arabs were not going to have it all their own way. Then the real blow fell. Having got Allenby's blessing for the transfer of Ali's and Abdulla's regular units, he went to Jidda to see Hussein. But the old man got wind of his coming and, on the pretext of Ramadhan, the Moslem month of fasting, took refuge in Mecca, where no "infidel" could follow him. Lawrence telephoned him from Jidda to try and pin him down to a decision but the Sherif refused to commit himself.

Envious and jealous of Feisal's success and suspicious of his close involvement with the British, Hussein's evasions made one thing very clear—he was not going to lift a finger to help put him into Damascus and was conserving all his strength to promote the interests of Ali and Abdulla, whom he had respectively named as heir-apparent to the kingdom of Hejaz and king of Syria. Feisal and this English adviser of his were pursuing a policy entirely contrary to his desires and he would have no part of it.

Blinded by jealousy and suspicion, the foolish old man could not see that his policy was bound to play straight into the hands of the French who, far more than the British whom he suspected so deeply, were determined to annex Syria and to grab whatever they could lay their hands on of liberated Arabia. Indeed, as Lawrence suspected on that grim day in Jidda, the Grand Sherif's suspicions were the direct result of French intrigues. Was it not Bremond who had got at Abdulla and put him against the British? And, while Feisal was out of the way, was it not obvious that Abdulla had poisoned his father against him and his British allies, using the rumours of the Anglo-French deal to wrap up Arabia to reinforce his bitter arguments?

Still worse was to follow. Within two months the Grand Sherif went from passive obstruction of Feisal to active sabotage of his efforts and incitement to mutiny among his soldiers. One day in August Feisal received a royal proclamation from Mecca, naming Jaafar Pasha the General Officer Commanding the Arab Northern Army, a rank which could only be held by Feisal himself. Jaafar, much embarrassed at being dragged into this family feud, offered to resign, but the Emir refused him and telegraphed to Mecca, protesting at his father's attempt to strip him of his command because of an unworthy jealousy and unfounded suspicions against him and his Syrian commanders.

In reply he received a telegram calling him a traitor and an outlaw. Feisal then offered his own resignation and the Sherif appointed Zeid to succeed him; but his unambitious youngest son promptly refused the nomination. It was imperative to fill the vacuum with all speed, there being only a few weeks left to get the Arab advance under way. Allenby was asked to intervene and to decide whether Feisal should carry on in defiance of his father's edicts or proclaim himself independent of Mecca. For several anxious days everybody waited while Allenby used pressure on Hussein to reinstate Feisal and the cable lines from the Holy City hummed with abusive cypher messages for Feisal which Lawrence, in a desperate effort to keep the temperature down, managed to garble before they were seen by the Emir. During this period a mutiny broke out among the Arab regulars who had heard rumours of the crisis and had interpreted Feisal's temporary withdrawal from circulation as evidence that he had deserted. This was only brought under control after Lawrence had produced the Emir and reminded them that "their faces were turned towards Damascus, not Mecca."

Finally, Hussein was persuaded to withdraw his mischievous proclamation. But, in the telegram to Feisal announcing this, he could not resist repeating all his accusations of treachery against himself and the Sherifian family. Once again Lawrence suppressed the offensive passages in the message before giving it to Feisal. "The telegraph has saved all our honour," the Emir exclaimed. Then in a whisper to Lawrence, "I mean the honour of nearly all of us." Thus the incident ended in laughter; but its portent was all too clear. The splendid mosaic of a united Arabia, which Feisal and Lawrence had tried to piece together with so much care, precision and diplomacy from so many jagged and conflicting tribal fragments, was beginning to fall apart. At the very moment when a joint Arab movement on Damascus was most imperative, if the Sherifian army was to establish itself as the liberator of Syria and Feisal as the rightful occupant of its throne, the whole Arab movement seemed to be breaking into rival factions under the divisive influences of internecine envy.

Lawrence returned to Cairo a bitterly disillusioned man. His enthusiasm had turned to cynicism; his sense of mission and his high personal ambition had gone sour as too much wine on the morrow of a night of intoxication.

21

Back at G.H.Q. Lawrence threw himself into the work of preparing for the combined British-Arab drive on Damascus. This was to include elaborate deception plans in the Jordan valley where dummy concentrations of vehicles, tents and aircraft would lead the Turks to expect that Allenby was attacking again from Jericho towards Salt and Amman, whereas his real intention was to go up the coast in an out-flanking movement. The Arabs were to help keep the Turks on the hop in the Jordan-Amman sector with an enveloping movement at Deraa—"the navel of the Turkish armies"—on 16th September, three days before the start of the main British advance. Since Feisal's army would not be ready until September, it was agreed that the surviving battalion of the Imperial Camel Corps under Colonel Buxton should be dispatched forthwith on a series of raiding operations against the Hejaz railway from Mudauwra to Amman. This would keep up the pressure on the Turks, while allowing time for the Arab striking force to concentrate itself at Azrak for the march against Deraa.

After guiding Buxton's men as far as the Wadi Rumm to instruct them in the ways and customs of the Arab tribes that they would meet on their expedition, Lawrence was flown to Feisal's camp in the plain of Jefer, north-east of Maan. The place was throbbing with activity and excitement—activity that betokened preparations for the coming march, excitement resulting from the visit of Nuri Shaalan who had come at last to pledge the active support of the Ruwalla. Lawrence was caught up in all this stimulating commotion, but he could no longer rejoice in the talk of national freedom that filled the Emir's tents. Although the final cause of his disenchantment lay with the Arabs, it was upon himself that he turned to vent his remorse and indignation. "As for honour, had I not lost that a year ago when I assured the Arabs that England kept her plighted word?"

Torn by a spiritual ambivalence, feeling a traitor to the cause he had embraced, and racked with doubt of the Arabs' ability to triumph over treachery, he listened to a Feisal daily preaching to the tribal chiefs as he might have listened to a play. No longer was he one of the principals, but a spectator watching and waiting while the actors on the stage played out their parts to the inevitable end of tragedy.

Among the Arabs I was the disillusioned, the sceptic, who envied them their cheap belief. The unperceived sham looked so well-fitting and becoming a dress for shoddy man. The ignorant, the superficial, the deceived were the happy among us. By our swindle they were glorified. . . . They were our dupes, wholeheartedly fighting the enemy. They blew before our intentions like chaff, being not chaff, but the bravest, simplest and merriest of men.

At this point the dagger of doubt piercing Lawrence's tormented brain was given another twist. Dawnay had arrived with news of Buxton's successful capture of Mudauwra and with a warning from Allenby to Feisal not to rush on to Damascus until he was certain that the British had broken through the Turkish defences. Feisal replied with a smile "that he would try this autumn for Damascus though the heavens fell, and, if the British were not able to carry their share of the attack, he would save his own

people by making a separate peace with Turkey."
Lawrence had known for some time that Feisal was
corresponding with Jemal Pasha; but in his Byzantine
way, he had regarded these exchanges not as treachery
but as a means of dividing the Turkish General Staff,
a section of which—a pan-Islamic group—were
bitterly opposed to their German ally and were re-
puted to believe in a measure of autonomy for the
Hejaz and might be ready to extend this to other
Arab provinces of the Ottoman empire. The contact
had started after Allenby's defeat at Salt, when Abd el
Kader's brother Mohammed Said had come as Jemal's
emissary to sound Feisal out on the possibility of a
negotiated settlement. Jemal, realizing that his strong
card was the Sykes-Picot agreement, laid much stress
on the need for all true Moslems to band together
to keep out the western infidels. But Feisal had sent
his emissary back with the rejoinder that he would call
off the fight only "if Turkey evacuated Amman and
handed over its province to Arab keeping." Jemal
had nearly hanged Mohammed Said for his failure to
do better than this and from then on, although the
correspondence continued fairly regularly, Feisal had
steadily returned nothing but tendentious answers to
every Turkish feeler. Lawrence had wisely fore-
warned him of the Anglo-French deal and had, so he
believed, convinced him that his best course was not
to make a separate peace with Turkey, but to prove
himself so loyal an ally to the British that they could
not, for shame, deny him the pledges they had made
to his father. Now even this belief was crumbling
and his chosen prophet and king was threatening to do a deal with the enemy. The nightmare was
closing in on him and the loneliness of not knowing
whom to trust nor whom to blame for the humiliating
fraud that he was perpetrating was becoming hideously
oppressive.

To cleanse his mind he decided to go with Joyce
and an armoured car company to reconnoitre the
area of Azrak, where Feisal's striking force was to

assemble for the final offensive. On this expedition Lawrence found a solace among the simple soldiers of the armoured car unit that was to shape the last dozen years of his life. His equals or his superiors in rank he could not resist treating with an infuriating arrogance, reminding them constantly of his intellectual superiority. But with his inferiors he was more at ease, although not one of these men that he met in the desert armoured cars during the war or in the Royal Air Force afterwards possessed one-hundredth part of his knowledge and education. With them he had no need to show off in order to rise above the sense of inferiority and freakishness which had haunted him from the day when he first learned of his illegitimate birth. Among such simple folk, were they Arabs or Englishmen, he found a natural easy-going acceptance of himself as that which, once the bladder of ambition had been pricked, the deepest part of his nature wished he could have been—a man like any other man. This was to be the escape from himself, from the fraud and the responsibility that he now felt he could no longer continue.

The agony of his soul at this point is beautifully portrayed in the words of his soliloquy written from memory of his thirtieth birthday on 16th August 1918 which he spent with the armoured car unit and Buxton's Camel Corps at the wells of Bair, waiting for the signal for the final advance.

It came to me queerly how from years ago I had meant to be a general and knighted when thirty. Such temporal dignities . . . were now in my grasp —only that my sense of the falsity of the Arab position cured me of my crude ambition: while it left me craving for good repute among men. This craving made me profoundly suspect my truthfulness to myself. Only too good an actor could so impress his favourable opinion. Here were the Arabs believing me, Allenby and Clayton trusting me, my bodyguard dying for me: and I began to wonder if all established reputations were founded, like mine, on fraud. . . . With men I had a sense always of being out of depth. This led to elaboration—the vice of amateurs tentative in their arts. . . . On this birthday in Bair, to satisfy my sense of sincerity, I began to dissect my beliefs and motives. . . . There was my craving to be liked—so strong and nervous that never could I open myself friendly to another. The terror of failure in an effort so important made me shrink from trying. . . . There was a craving to be famous; and a horror of being known to like being known. Contempt for my passion for distinction made me refuse every offered honour. . . . I liked the things underneath me and took my pleasures and adventures downward. There seemed a certainty in degradation, a final safety. . . . True there lurked always that Will uneasily waiting to burst out . . . self-seeking ambitions visited me, but not to stay, since my critical self would make me fastidiously reject their fruits. . . . When a thing lay within my reach, I no longer wanted it; my delight lay in the desire . . . when a desire gained head, I used to strive until I had just to open my hand and take it. Then I would turn away, content that it had been within my strength. . . . Indeed, the truth was I did not like the "myself" I could see and hear.

So critical a piece of self-evaluation may seem somewhat over-dramatized. But this was the high point of drama and disillusionment and Lawrence was nearing the end of his mental tether. The weight of responsibility had suddenly become almost unendurable, now that the dream of personal achievement was fading. He had endured every mental anguish, physical pain, and spiritual torment so long as the prospect held of an Arab strength sufficient to win freedom after victory. Now he was afraid to carry on with the responsibility of leading—or misleading— these too weak and simple people to exchange one alien rule for another. Now he yearned to abdicate.

> It was part of my failure never to have found a
> chief to use me. All of them . . . allowed me too
> free a hand . . . gave me licence which I abused in
> insipid indulgence. . . . Feisal was a brave, weak,
> ignorant spirit, trying to do work for which only a
> genius, a prophet or a great criminal was fitted.
> . . . Allenby came nearest to my longings for a
> master, but I had to avoid him . . . lest he show
> feet of clay with that friendly word which must
> shatter my allegiance.

In these twilight hours of the mind Lawrence was
very near to the brink of insanity. He had driven
himself for too long beyond the limits of what even
his brain and body could tolerate. The end was
now inevitable—a hollow victory and a mortified
withdrawal. The only question was whether he could
endure that far.

22

A week before the start of Allenby's offensive a vast congregation of Arabs was poised at Azrak for the final spring. Feisal with his five hundred regular troops under Nuri es Said, plus Pisani's artillerymen and elements of the Egyptian Camel Corps under Peake, had been joined by Auda, Nuri Shaalan, Sherif Nasir, Fahad, Adhub, Talal, Mohammed el Dheilan and a host of lesser sheikhs, with several thousands of supporting tribesmen from the Howeitat, Ruwalla, Zebn and Serahin who in turn were swelled by Druses from the hills of Syria and townsmen from the north. Lawrence had arrived by armoured car with Joyce, Young and two new officers, Stirling and Winterton, and a British contingent of forty drivers and machine-gunners. Two aeroplanes had been flown up from Akaba, biplanes held together by wire and spit and piloted by two intrepid aviators Murphy and Junor, renowned for their hair-raising exploits against the Turkish air defences.

The plan for encircling Deraa consisted of a three-pronged attack on the railways leading out of the town, which were to be kept cut for at least a week to immobilize the Turks and prevent their armies in Jordan and Syria hastening to the support of the Palestine front when the Allies attacked. Not having enough air cover to risk a direct assault on Deraa to destroy the railway junction, they decided first to blow up the railway to the south to cut off Amman. (Buxton's Camel Corps had been detailed to do this in their previous sweep from Mudauwra but had been prevented by superior Turkish forces.) Then they would move north and blow the Damascus line and finally finish up with the line to Palestine.

The daring of this operation is difficult to imagine. Everything depended upon the success of Allenby's attack and this in its turn depended upon the extent to which the Turks could be made to believe that the main Allied offensive would be directed against Deraa. If the Arabs failed to create the necessary diversion to achieve this deception or if Allenby failed to break through in the west, Feisal's army would be caught like rats in a trap. They were operating several hundreds of miles inside the Turkish lines with their line of retreat threatened by the enemy garrisons that still remained intact at Maan and Amman. With overwhelmingly superior forces at both these places and at Deraa all the enemy had to do, if the plan failed, was to close in from the north and south and cut Feisal's Arabs to pieces.

Nobody knew better than Lawrence the extent of this mortal gamble upon which he and the Arabs were engaged. But his mood on arriving at Azrak could scarcely have been more disenchanted, even disinterested. In contrast to his exhilaration on the march to Wejh and the long trek to Akaba, he could not even work up any enthusiasm over the gay and expectant atmosphere of Feisal's camp. "Everyone was stout and in health. Except myself . . . I was tired to death of these Arabs; petty incarnate semites . . . they realised our absolute in their unrestrained capacity for good and evil; and for two years I had profitably shammed to be their companion! Today it came to me with finality that my patience as regards the false position I had been led into was finished. . . ."

With some relief he sat back and let Joyce make the decisions. Peake was despatched to do the demolition work with his Camel Corps contingent, who had been turned into sappers for the purpose. But, as Lawrence was preparing to leave the next day with

the main body for the advance base at Umtaiye, a few
miles south of Deraa, word came that the demoli-
tioners had been held up by hostile Arabs near
to the spot selected to cut the Amman railway. Wear-
ily Lawrence gathered himself up and with Joyce and
Winterton and a couple of armoured cars dashed off
to do the job himself. Rushing the Turkish block-
house, they wiped out all but five of the defenders and
blew up an eighty-foot bridge to seal off Deraa's
communications with the south. Returning from this
raid they were nearly captured by an enemy patrol,
when the Rolls-Royce tender broke down and was
only going again with the utmost difficulty before the
raiders ran out of ammunition keeping the enemy at
bay.

Something happened to Lawrence at the time of this
raid which was to change him from the indifferent
spectator that he had been at Azrak into a frenzied
partisan, who for the next two weeks fought and
killed like a man in the throes of some diabolical
delirium. Perhaps this fresh encounter with the enemy
had caused all his suppressed rage at his treatment
in Deraa to boil over in the cauldron of his angry
soul; or perhaps it was a reaction to the utter futility
that he now felt about his mission; or it might simply
have been a reflex of the spirit threshing wildly in a
last desperate convulsion. Lawrence himself gave no
explanation of the transformation. But, when he
rejoined the main body of Nuri es Said's regulars
marching to the north of Deraa, there was a wild
glint in his eye that presaged a violence and hatred
altogether out of keeping with the gentle spirit that
had once set so great a store on sparing and saving
life. Despair had turned to rage and he had become a
killer, no longer restraining and even encouraging
the Bedouin in the satisfaction of the blood-feud. Indeed his recklessness in the engagements that followed
during the next two or three days almost suggested
a suicidal intent. Never before had he exposed himself

so daringly or taken quite such hazardous operations upon himself.

In the march around the eastern side of Deraa he made little attempt to conceal his movements, advancing almost within sight of the town, which was defended by three thousand troops, including German and Austrian units. At any minute his column of a few hundred men could have been spotted by the ever-active Turkish air patrols and wiped out by an enemy sortie in strength. But the enemy stayed within his gates deceived by wild rumours that he was about to be besieged by eighteen thousand well-armed Arabs. The spot where Lawrence chose to blow up the Deraa-Damascus line was a bridge perilously near the town, only six miles to the north. But again luck was with him, for the Turks had not thought that anyone could be so daring as to attack so near to Deraa and had not strengthened their guard-posts. With the aid of Pisani's shells, the Arabs attacked the post defending the bridge and massacred all its occupants. Then, in the middle of the subsequent demolitions of the track, the Turks attacked with bombers and one of the two fighter aeroplanes brought up from Akaba was shot down in an heroic attempt by its pilot, Junor, to break up the enemy formation.

Lawrence eventually finished the demolition job himself and, having posted a small section of troops and guns to guard his retreat and to harass any Turkish attempts to repair the damage, pressed on to complete the task of isolating Deraa by destroying the line to Haifa and the means of reinforcement for the Turkish 7th and 8th Armies about to face the full onslaught of Allenby's offensive. It was now 17th September, two days before zero hour for the final Allied push. By this time the enemy was thoroughly alarmed and, just as Allenby and Lawrence had planned, suspected that all this furious activity portended a major Allied assault against Deraa. Liman von Sanders, the German general who had been sent to stiffen Turkish resistance in Palestine, was completely fooled by the combination of Lawrence's diversionary attacks on the railways and the siting of dummy British concentrations in the Jordan valley and promptly dispatched reinforcements to the Deraa sector.

No sooner had these troops reached their destination than Lawrence sprang the trap that was to bottle them up in Deraa. For the completion of this exercise he chose two targets—first, the station at Mezerib, and second, the Yarmuk bridge that had escaped destruction in the previous November. With his bodyguard and a group of tribesmen, plus a detachment of Nuri es Said's regulars and Pisani's artillerymen who were rapidly learning to be anti-aircraft gunners under the ever increasing Turkish aerial bombing and machine-gun attacks, he marched on Mezerib and captured the station after a brief barrage of gunfire had killed most of the defenders. Then, leaving the tribesmen to loot their fill, he pressed on to deal with the bridge. This time he hoped to take the viaduct by guile, the captain of the Turkish guard-post being an Armenian anxious to do anything he could to damage the hated Turks. But the plan miscarried, when the captain was arrested on suspicion of treason, and Lawrence moved on to an alternative target, another high-spanned bridge over the Yarmuk river.

The Turks were there in strength and, although Pisani's guns succeeded in destroying their redoubt, they retired to a row of trenches along the railway embankment, from where they continued to pour a murderous fire on the raiders. Lawrence's demolition team were afraid to go forward carrying explosives under so heavy a fire, knowing that one bullet in the gelignite would blow them to pieces. But his bodyguard were game enough and, with their aid, he managed to lay charges, piling the gelignite against the tall piers of the viaduct. Since this bridge, incidentally Lawrence's seventy-ninth, was "strategically the most critical, since we were going to live opposite it at

Umtaiye until Allenby came forward and relieved us," he made a very complete job of its demolition and, when the explosion came, eight hundred pounds of gelignite blew up in one burst, leaving nothing but a yawning pit and a mass of broken twisted girders lying in the gorge below.

Lawrence had accomplished with twenty-four hours to spare the essential preliminaries for Allenby's offensive. Deraa was now cut off from the north, south and west and there could be no possibility of Turkish movement by rail into or out of Palestine. The Turkish armies facing the Allies must now either stand firm or be annihilated, for there was no longer any line of retreat left open nor any means of rapid reinforcement.

Lawrence's job was in fact done and his orders were to await further developments. But, gripped as he now was by a maniacal fervour, he could not stop and retire quietly east of Deraa to wait upon the British advance. This was the last burst of his strength and he must go on till it left him. "A week, two weeks, three and I would insist upon relief. My nerve had broken; and I would be lucky if the ruin of it could be hidden so long," he had reflected at Azrak as Feisal's forces gathered for the envelopment of Deraa. He knew that when he did stop, it would be for good. Whatever the consequences he must see Feisal into Damascus; then he would ask to be relieved of further responsibilities in Arabia.

23

The news that greeted Lawrence on his return to Umtaiye made it clear that he would not have to wait much longer for his relief. A courier aeroplane had arrived from Palestine with messages from the Commander-in-Chief announcing that, in the first two days of their offensive, the Allies had broken through and smashed the Turkish 7th and 8th Armies to pieces; Nablus and Haifa had been taken and the enemy was retreating northwards in complete disorder. Nasir and Talal were present to hear the joyous tidings and, vocally supported by the tribesmen, clamoured for an immediate Arab march on Damascus. But Lawrence, who bore the scars of Turkish bomb splinters from the enemy's all too persistent attempts to break up their recent railway operations, felt that the Arab army must have more air support if it was going to fight its way to Damascus against the Turkish air force. Hopping a lift on the courier aeroplane, he hastened to Allenby's headquarters, where he found the Commander-in-Chief unmoved, almost bored, by the success of his offensive. Palestine was his, and now to the next business, was his matter-of-fact attitude.

The next business, he informed Lawrence, was to consist of three thrusts—one to Amman by General Chaytor's New Zealand division, one to Deraa by the Indian division under General Barrow and one to Kuneitra, between the Sea of Galilee and Damascus, by the Australians under General Chauvel. Lawrence's orders were to assist these three attacks but

"I was not to carry out my saucy threat to take Damascus, till we were all together." This gave Lawrence his opportunity to ask for air support. Graphically he described the harassments which he and his demolition force had suffered as they dynamited their way around Deraa. At their advance base at Umtaiye they were living in a hornet's nest, surrounded by Turkish airfields; and their smallest move would be spotted by enemy observer planes and then attacked by bombs and machine-gun fire. They had tried to destroy the airfields and the aeroplanes by raids at night but without success. If they were to advance in open order in support of the Allies' three thrusts towards Damascus, air cover was imperative.

Allenby listened attentively with his air force commanders, Salmond and Borton, who when Lawrence had finished his plea promised two Bristol fighters and a Handley Page bomber converted as a transport plane to ferry petrol and spares for the fighters' maintenance. Little though this may sound today, it was enough for Lawrence, who returned to Umtaiye well satisfied with his errand and appreciative of what he considered to be generous treatment from his British superiors. His only recorded reservation about this encounter concerned, needless to say, his orders to wait for the Allies before entering Damascus.

Allenby's attack not only broke the two Turkish armies in Palestine; it also forced the withdrawal of Jemal Pasha's 4th Army from east of the Jordan. Lawrence's instructions were to harass and contain these Turkish forces until the New Zealanders drove them out of Amman, and then to cut them up as they retreated towards Deraa and Damascus. But, after blowing up yet another long stretch of the Amman-Deraa line to ensure that there could be no possible retreat northwards by rail, he abandoned the enemy to the attentions of the local tribes and hurried off towards Deraa itself to keep up the pressure on the Turks and prevent any possibility of their regrouping as a rearguard.

With Auda, Nuri Shaalan, Talal, Nasir and Nuri es Said and a force which had now been swelled by a further influx of Ruwalla tribesmen to four thousand men, he retraced his steps of the previous week, first to the north and then, after more railway demolitions on the Damascus line, to the west of Deraa. On the way Auda, Talal and Nuri Shaalan led raiding parties to test the strength of the remaining Turkish garrisons between Deraa and Damascus, each one returning to report the capture of hundreds of demoralized Turks. Messages were also dropped from aeroplanes that Barrow's Indians and Chauvel's Australian division were driving thousands of Turks before them.

Then a message arrived for Talal that the Germans in Deraa were setting fire to their aeroplanes and stores in preparation to evacuate the place, a report which their own eyes could confirm from the thick black clouds of smoke that could be seen belching from the town. But Talal's thoughts were not on Deraa at this point. He had worked out from the reports of the Turks retreating before the Indians that their route would lie through Tafas, his own village. The enemy column was estimated to number two thousand and he was worried for the safety of his people. Lawrence readily agreed to his pleas to ride with all speed and try to head the Turks off and take them prisoner before they reached Tafas. Half way there they heard that they were too late. A group of Arabs whom they met on the road told them that the column was already entering Tafas. The Arabs were driving before them a bunch of miserable Turkish prisoners, whose naked backs were blue with bruises from the merciless beating of their captors. But on learning that these Turks were members of the police in Deraa at whose hands he, and many others, had suffered the most appalling iniquities, Lawrence could feel no pity and left the Arabs to do their worst.

Maybe he also had, like Talal, some premonition of what he would find in Tafas after the Turks had been through it. Certainly the scene that confronted them as they rode into the village could hardly have been more horrifying. The Turks had indulged themselves in an orgy of atrocities. The village had been burned and all its inhabitants, including women and children, had been butchered.

The village lay stilly under its slow wreaths of white smoke, as we rode near on our guard. Some grey heaps seemed to hide in the long grass, embracing the ground in the close way of corpses. We looked away from these, knowing they were dead; but from one a little figure tottered off, as if to escape us. It was a child, three or four years old, whose dirty smock was stained red over one shoulder and side, with blood from a large half-fibrous wound, perhaps a lance thrust, just where neck and body joined. . . . We rode past the other bodies of men and women and four more dead babies. . . . By the outskirts were low mud walls, sheepfolds, and on one something red and white. I looked close and saw the body of a woman folded across it, bottom upwards, nailed there by a saw bayonet whose haft stuck hideously into the air from between her naked legs. She had been pregnant, and about her lay others, perhaps twenty in all, variously killed, but set out in accord with an obscene taste.

Talal had seen enough. With a moan like a wounded beast, he drew his headcloth about his face and charged headlong after the retreating Turks whose column had only just left the scene of carnage and was still visible from the village. It was a magnificent last gesture. The Turks, amazed to see this lone figure galloping at them, stopped dead in their tracks. Then a few yards from the astonished enemy Talal, still galloping furiously, rose in his stirrups and shouted his war cry "Talal, Talal!" In the next second the Turks opened fire with rifles and machine-guns

and the gallant old outlaw fell dead at their feet,
ripped through with bullets.

Auda and Lawrence had witnessed the whole
scene and, when it was over, the Howeitat leader
grimly intoned, "God give him mercy; we will take
his price." Lawrence turned to his men. Any hesitation he had ever felt about wanton killing had
gone. Now he could only think of vengeance, of
slaughter for slaughter, of butchery for butchery;
the flame of the blood-feud possessed him. "The
best of you brings me the most Turkish dead," he
said; and, with that, he and his Arabs went to work
to wipe out the butchers of Tafas. By Lawrence's
express orders no prisoners were taken.

Catching up with the retreating Turkish column,
the Arabs fell upon them. "In a madness born of
the horror of Tafas we killed and killed, even blowing in the heads of the fallen and of the animals;
as though their death and running blood could
slake our agony." Only one section of two hundred Turks were taken prisoner by a group of
Arabs who had not heard their leader's order. Lawrence was about to spare these men when a nearby
commotion revealed a wounded Arab who had
been pinned to the ground "like a collected insect"
with bayonets driven through his legs and shoulders.
He had just enough life in him to say that the
men now prisoners were responsible for his tor-
tures, whereupon Lawrence gave the order to
shoot them where they stood with machine-guns.

By sunset the desperate battle was over and almost every one of the two thousand Turks who
had entered Tafas the day before had been slaugh-
tered—at the express orders of the gentle archaeologist who despised the soldier's profession and who
not many months earlier had bitterly attacked a
British fellow officer for making light of twenty
casualties at the capture of Wejh. Such were the
depths of the nightmare in which he was now en-
gulfed. "God will give you peace," Farraj had

said to him as he died. But it was not to be, at least until many years later. Indeed, if in these last days of the desert war he was able to see into his soul through the blood-red haze that clouded his mind and transformed his character, he must have been among the most tortured of God's creatures.

24

The rout of the Turkish armies was now complete
and, at dawn on the morrow of the Tafas massacre,
Lawrence entered Deraa to find Sherif Nasir already installed in the mayor's house in the wake
of the retreating enemy. Nasir had also taken a
terrible toll of the Turkish and German columns
evacuating Deraa. Of the eight regiments that broke
out of the town on 27th September more than two-
thirds were massacred before they could reach Damascus.

While Lawrence was rehearsing Nasir in his duties as the new overlord of Deraa, word came that
General Barrow's division was approaching the
town. Lawrence rode out to meet the general, narrowly escaping being shot by some trigger-happy
Australians of the advance guard, who mistook
him and his reception party for a band of Arab
marauders. Barrow greeted Lawrence stiffly and
was rewarded, according to one eyewitness, with
a typical mixture of schoolboy impudence and om-
niscient superiority, with liberal references to his
intimate association with General Allenby thrown
in for good measure. Barrow, a stiff professional
soldier, resented this treatment by an upstart major
very much junior to him in rank and years. Lawrence equally had no use for Barrow, who regarded
the Arabs as a conquered people and capable only
of responding to the goadings of fear.

As they rode together into Deraa, Barrow made
it clear that his troops would take over the town's

administration and seemed surprised and put out when, as he enumerated the various things that must be done for health and good order, Lawrence was able to say that each one had been taken care of. Barrow then turned to the next phase— the entry into Damascus. He was to leave the next day to join up with Chauvel and the Australians so that they should enter the city together. Patronizingly he offered that Lawrence and his Arabs might accompany him as his right flank. But Lawrence had other ideas; and one of them was to move Feisal up from Azrak to Deraa in preparation for the last dash ahead of the Allied advance.

Auda and his tribesmen, Nuri Shaalan and the Ruwalla and Sherif Nasir had gone ahead in pursuit of the last remnants of the Turkish 4th Army, a ragged column of two thousand men desperately trying to ward off the flank attacks of the Arabs with the few mountain guns that they had been able to salvage from their abandoned posts. Although the defeated Turks were scarcely in a position to inflict further damage upon anyone, the tribesmen could not resist the prospect of plunder and pressed their attacks until all two thousand had been either killed or taken prisoner. Auda, in particular, "killed and killed, plundered and captured till dawn showed him the end." Then, the last battle over and the blood-feud against the hated Turk requited, he and his friends retired to Kiswe, a few miles south of Damascus, where General Chauvel's Australians were awaiting the arrival of Barrow's Indian division.

Lawrence joined the old warrior that night at Kiswe. For one who for two years had planned and dreamed only of the day when he and his King would enter Damascus in triumph, this eve of victory should have been a night of intoxicating expectancy. In fact it was very different. Instead of being proud and excited, he felt abandoned and ashamed. As he moved about the camp, unnoticed by the British and Australian troops, he felt suddenly and painfully the utter loneliness and incongruity of his position.

In the night my colour was unseen. I could walk as I pleased, an unconsidered Arab: and this finding myself among, but cut off from, my own kin made me strangely alone. . . . About the soldiers hung the Arabs: gravely-gazing men from another sphere. My crooked duty had banished me among them for two years. Tonight I was nearer to them than to the troops, and I resented it, as shameful.

❖   ❖   ❖

That same night—30th September 1918—the last remnants of the Turkish and German garrisons withdrew from Damascus and, as their rearguard filed dejectedly past the Town Hall, the Arab flag was hoisted by the members of Feisal's Damascus committee. Nasir and Nuri Shaalan were itching to march into the city the same evening but Lawrence dissuaded them. Enough of the brilliant stage-manager remained in him to convince them that it would be far more impressive if the sheikhs entered Damascus with Feisal and himself "serenely at dawn" the following day. He had only one day in hand before the Australians would move in and he was resolved to make the most of it.

As the column moved off in the pale light of the dawn, led by Nasir in honour of his fifty battles with the enemy, a galloping horseman rode out from the city. He had been sent by Shukri el Ayubi, the leader of the Damascus resistance committee, with whom Feisal had made contact the night before. With a joyous salutation to Feisal and Lawrence, the messenger held out to them a bunch of yellow grapes. "Good news; Damascus salutes you."

Then, as they neared the city's approaches, a strange welcome met them, the silent greeting of a people too stunned by the suddenness of their liberation to voice their feelings. "The way was packed with people lined solid on the sidewalks, in the road, at the windows and on the balconies or house-tops. Many were crying, a few cheered faintly, some bolder ones cried our names: but mostly they looked and looked, joy shining in their eyes." But once inside Damascus the tears of silent joy turned to wild rejoicing as a swirling mob shrieked its welcome—"Feisal, Aurens, Nasir"— and danced and sang and pressed upon the cars that bore their king and liberator to his capital. Dervishes ran before them, slashing their flesh in frenzy. Roar upon roar of cheers crashed along the streets and across the squares of the city like surf rising with the storm. For a moment Lawrence almost forgot his fears for the future, as fleetingly he dreamed once more that all this united rejoicing might prove to have a sufficient strength behind it to establish Feisal and his Arabs as masters of their own destiny.

But the dream was short-lived. At the Town Hall Nasir and Nuri Shaalan had already arrived and were seated in the Council's ante-chamber when Lawrence finally managed to squeeze his way through the milling mass of Damascenes that surrounded the seat of government. To Lawrence's dumb amazement there also sat on either side of these two trusted friends none other than the traitorous Emir Abd el Kader and his brother Mohammed Said, Jemal Pasha's tool in his attempt to suborn Feisal. Before Lawrence could recover himself, Mohammed Said stepped forward and announced that he, his brother and Shukri had formed a government of liberation and had proclaimed Hussein of Mecca "King of the Arabs."

Dumbfounded by this statement, Lawrence turned
to Shukri, hoping for a denial. But the old man
could only confirm that the Algerians—religious
fanatics, most of them—had taken control of his
committee by force. He held them in as great contempt as Lawrence, for had he not seen for himself how they stood by the Turks until they had
run away. But what could he do? He was not
strong enough to resist them. Lawrence could feel
no bitterness towards Shukri for his capitulation.
He had kept going during the Turkish occupation,
despite what he had suffered at Jemal's hands, and
now he was at the end of his tether.

Yet somebody must try to spike this treachery:
Lawrence turned desperately to Nasir to give a
lead. At that moment the room was filled by the
roar of a familiar voice and the throng of Arabs in
the antechamber became suddenly silent and then
parted to reveal Auda tearing at a Druse Sheikh,
who had insulted him and for whose blood the old
warrior was shouting like a maniac. When after a
struggle the two were dragged apart and the Druse
was hustled out of the Town Hall, Lawrence looked
around for Nasir; but he had gone, wheedled
away by the Algerians, leaving Lawrence in the
middle of a howling multitude of Arabs, Druses,
Damascenes, Bedouin tribesmen and peasants—
delirious with the sudden victory that had come
upon them, shouting the names of their own special heroes and leaders, fighting each other with
their fists. So this was the united Arabia for which
he, and they, had fought—a cry now drowned in
this babbling of fools, a throne threatened by
usurpers.

Bitterly Lawrence set about the business of saving Damascus for Feisal. He sent for Abd el Kader
and his brother. At first they refused his sum-
mons; then a while later they relented, only to
find themselves confronted by Nuri es Said with
a detachment of his regulars and Nuri Shaalan

with a threatening group of his Ruwalla tribesmen. Lawrence then announced that, acting on behalf of the Emir Feisal, he had abolished Abd el Kader's government and had appointed in its place Shukri el Ayubi as Acting Governor and Nuri es Said as military commander. Mohammed Said immediately challenged this action, denounced Lawrence as an infidel Britisher and called on Nasir to assert his authority. But the Sherif "could only sit and look miserable at this falling out of friends." Abd el Kader then tried a more direct attack, drawing his dagger with a volley of oaths against the Englishman who had thwarted his plans. But old Auda was on him like a flash. Foiled in his attempt to wash out the insult in the Town Hall in Druse blood, his gorge was up and he was spoiling for a fight. But Abd el Kader withdrew before the old man could strike him and with his brother at his heels beat an indignant and hasty retreat from the meeting place.

When they had gone, Lawrence and the others got down to the practical problems of restoring government and order to the city. A police force had to be organized and a fire brigade set up; the electricity supply had to be got going; sanitation arrangements had to be made and the streets cleared of corpses, broken-down wrecks of Turkish cars and carts and other sundry debris of war; food and relief had to be brought in for a population that had been half-starved for days; the hospitals had to be cleaned up and medical supplies imported to cope with outbreaks of typhus and dysentery; and communications, rail and telegraph, had to be restored. They worked like fiends through almost all of the night, determined to be able to show the Allied troops when they arrived the next day what they could do to govern themselves and bring order out of chaos. But, for Lawrence, the achievement was no more than a façade. The reality was in the scene he had witnessed in the Town Hall and in the intrigues which divided the Sherifian family.

As he finally closed his eyes to catch a little sleep after the long night of labour, he heard the muezzin chanting the call to prayer across the exultant torch-lit city. "Come to prayer, come to security. God alone is great; there is no God but God and Mohammed is his Prophet." Then, in a lowered voice, the muezzin added, "And He is very good to us this day, O people of Damascus." As the tumult of rejoicing hushed and the people obeyed the call to prayer and thanks-giving, Lawrence felt once again "loneliness and lack of reason in their movement: since, only for me, of all the hearers, was the event sorrowful and the phrase meaningless."

About an hour later Lawrence was wakened with the news that Abd el Kader was starting a rebellion. He had called a meeting of his men and of the Druses who, smarting under the new government's refusal to pay them for services which they claimed to have rendered, fell an easy prey to the Algerian's rantings that Feisal and his followers were stooges of the infidel English and must be removed if the Moslem faith was to be saved from corruption. Lawrence and Nuri es Said quickly made their dispositions to deal with the threatened rising. Nuri posted machine-gunners at strategic points while Lawrence, accompanied only by Kirkbride, went about the streets addressing the people on the subject of Feisal's loyalty and Abd el Kader's treachery to the Arab cause. It was a perilous mission and several times he was only saved from death at the hands of Druse fanatics, inflamed by Abd el Kader's propaganda, by the timely use of Kirkbride's revolver. Chauvel's Australians had just arrived when the rising started and the general at once offered the support of his troops to put it down. But, partly from pride, partly because he sensed it to be only a minor affray, Lawrence declined the offer; and, a few hours after the Arab machine-gunners had broken up the insurgents with one long rattle of fire, Abd el Kader fled from the city leaving his brother to be taken prisoner.

Lawrence was now at the point of exhaustion. He had had only three hours' sleep since leaving Deraa four days before. He had had to shoulder the burden of establishing Feisal and his government, of defeating the machinations of the would-be usurpers, of restoring civic government to a city abandoned in chaos by its former occupiers and, most difficult of all, of trying to make law-abiding citizens out of rebels, men who had spent years of their lives, and the last two years in particular, in defying authority and breaking every established law as their patriotic duty. It was a task beyond the power of any one man, let alone a man numbed by physical fatigue and on the verge of spiritual collapse.

Yet, there was still one more horror to be endured. At lunch on the second day in Damascus, an Australian army doctor asked Lawrence to do something about the Turkish hospital where the filth was beyond belief and the doctors and orderlies had all left. The doctor's description turned out to be no exaggeration. As Lawrence stepped inside he was met with

> a sickening stench and, as my eyes grew open, a sickening sight. The stone floor was covered with dead bodies, side by side, some in full uniform, some in underclothing, some stark naked. . . . They crept with rats who had gnawed wet red galleries into them. A few were corpses nearly fresh . . . others must have been there for long. Of some the flesh, going putrid, was yellow and blue and black. Many were already swollen twice or thrice life-width, their fat heads laughing with black mouths across jaws harsh with stubble. . . . A few had burst open and were liquescent with decay.

Inside the wards there was scarcely a sound from the long rows of still figures lying rigid on their pallets, "from which liquid muck had dripped down to stiffen on the cemented floor." These were the living, but not one had the strength to do more than groan for pity and wave their emaciated arms, "a thin fluttering like withered leaves, as they vainly fell back again upon their beds."

Lawrence and Kirkbride went in search of help. The Australians refused but some Turkish doctors were rounded up and, with the aid of a grave-digging party of Turkish prisoners, were put to the job of sorting out and burying the dead and cleaning up the wards and their still surviving occupants. Kirkbride supervised the burials and Lawrence, when he had received the tally from the doctors—fifty-six dead, two hundred dying and seven hundred injured or sick—went to get some rest, but not before General Chauvel had sought him out to register a complaint that some of the Arab troops had been slack about saluting his officers!

The following day conditions at the hospital bore no comparison with the filth that Lawrence had discovered. With Kirkbride standing over them, the doctors were cleaning up the place and appointing Turkish orderlies from among the prisoners to look after the sick. A lot, however, still remained to be done, and, as Lawrence was making his rounds of inspection, a major in the army medical corps came up to him and asked him if he was in charge.

"In a way, yes," replied Lawrence.

"Scandalous, disgraceful, outrageous, ought to be shot," the major exploded.

Lawrence was beyond the point of further endurance. As his nerve snapped under the sudden onslaught of this blimpish imbecile, he made no attempt to defend himself or explain how things had been the day before. Instead he burst into a cackling laugh.

"Bloody brute," bawled the major and, raising his hand, smacked Lawrence hard across the face.

As he stalked away, muttering something about barbarians lower than animals, Lawrence stood for a moment in contemplation. He could feel no anger with his attacker, only shame for himself and his spiritual uncleanliness.

But the blow had suddenly brought him back to his senses out of the semi-consciousness of exhaustion. In this moment he knew that he could carry on no longer, that neither his mind nor his body could be driven any further. Then, as he left the hospital, he recognized Allenby's Rolls-Royce outside the main hotel. Quickly he crossed the street and entered the hotel and in a few minutes was giving his final report to the Commander-in-Chief. Allenby listened attentively and in a few words confirmed all Lawrence's appointments and orders and laid down the spheres of responsibility for Feisal's administration and that of the Allied armies.

Then Lawrence asked for his release. Allenby at first refused to sanction it, arguing that his services would now be more than ever needed in Arabia. But it was no use; he knew Lawrence well enough to realize that his mind was made up. What had happened to bring about the change and why the victory had now turned sour which Lawrence had fought and worked and overtaxed himself to achieve, he probably never understood. But he liked and respected his extraordinary subordinate far too much to force him to stay against his will.

So Lawrence left the scene of his triumph as suddenly and with as little explanation of himself as he had first entered upon the adventure. At a moment when even his harshest critics were beginning to acclaim him as a genius, he felt nothing but shame for what he had done, for the sham that he had been and for the fraud that he had perpetrated on the friends who trusted him. Locked in the prison of his self-mortification all he could think of was escape.

25

No two of Lawrence's biographers seem to agree upon the reasons which lay behind this passion to escape from the scene of triumph. David Garnett holds that he left because he felt that the next round in the Arab drama would be fought at the conference table and that he would be more useful to his Arab friends if he hastened to London than if he stayed to gather the fruits of his own victory in Damascus. Lowell Thomas attributes his departure to physical and mental exhaustion and is supported by Dr. Ernest Altounyan, a naturalized British doctor and poet of Armenian origin and one of Lawrence's closest friends. Liddell Hart states that Lawrence told him, "it had finished, what better reason?" As for Lawrence's own explanation, he said that he had become so afraid of his desire for power and prestige that he had to escape.

They could all be right in their assessments, for there is no real contradiction between these explanations. Exhausted he certainly was and with good reason. Escaping from the shadow of his own ambition, yes too—his account of the last months of the desert campaign rings with the torment of a man who has seen the reflection of his soul in the mirror of self-analysis and been terrified by what he saw. At the same time his subsequent pleadings for the cause of Arab independence on his arrival in London and throughout the Peace Conference showed that he still wanted to be, and was, of service to his Arab friends outside Arabia. Equally Lawrence's task "had fin-

ished" in the Middle East. Sir Ronald Storrs in his
Orientations revealed that, towards the end of their
wartime association. Lawrence's relations with Feisal
had become soured and that afterwards Feisal had
spoken in ungratefully disparaging terms of his erstwhile guide and ally, "which," Storrs added, "I would
have resented more if I had ever imagined that
kings could like kingmakers." From this there can be
little doubt that, once in Damascus, Feisal made it
clear to Lawrence that his job in Arabia was done.
The king was on his throne; the kingmaker could now
be dismissed, should indeed be dismissed, if Feisal
was to clear himself of the suspicion prevailing in
Mecca that he was too greatly influenced by this
infidel Britisher.

❖   ❖   ❖

Lawrence, now promoted to Colonel, returned to
London and reported to the War Office a few days
before the general armistice in November 1918 proclaimed the final defeat of Germany and all her partners. No sooner had he arrived than he set to work
in the interests of Arab independence. Summoned before the Eastern Commission of the British Cabinet,
he submitted a memorandum in the most colourful
prose which related the origins and purposes of the
Arab Revolt and proposed a plan for the post-war
arrangement of Arabia. The Hejaz should have full
independence, he suggested. Mesopotamia should become a British mandate and Feisal should be given
virtually the whole of Syria save for a strip of coast
including Beirut, which should be conceded to France.
As to the Balfour Declaration of 1917, pledging a
national home for Jews in Palestine, he asserted
that the Arabs were agreeable provided that it should
be under British control and did not involve the
creation of a Jewish national state.

These views were by no means unpopular in British official circles at that time. For one thing, as Jean

Beraud Villars points out in his *T. E. Lawrence,*
Francophobia was rife in Britain at the end of World
War I. After four years of war and slaughter a large
proportion of the British army and nation had come to
believe that their sufferings "had been imposed on
them solely for the benefit for the French." For another, Britain was anything but keen on satisfying
French aims to expand in the Middle East. True, they
had been forced by the exigencies of war and the need
to sweeten their French allies into certain undertakings
to allow France to establish herself in the Levant
after the war was won. But, if France could be
bought off at the price suggested by Lawrence, this
should leave a clear field for British predominance
while at the same time honouring, in part at least,
Britain's pledges to Sherif Hussein. Also it was a
relief to hear from one so close to Feisal and so
knowledgeable about the aims of the Arabs that it
would be possible, without Arab opposition, to fulfil
Mr. Arthur Balfour's undertaking to the Zionist movement that the Jews—victims of so much brutality and
persecution in Eastern and Central Europe—would
be allowed under British protection to settle in the
Promised Land.

Yet, hardly had this self-satisfying mood settled on
Whitehall, than the first rumblings of trouble began
to make themselves heard in Damascus. Against
Lawrence's advice the Arabs had taken Beirut,
the principal centre of Christianity and French cul-
ture in the Levant, instead of leaving it to be lib-
erated by the Allies as one of the areas reserved to
French tutelage under the Sykes-Picot agreement.
With the arrival of Georges Picot, a relative of the
agreement's co-author, as High Commissioner for
Syria, the territory was handed over to the French on
the orders of the British Commander-in-Chief. But the
French authorities were not to be so easily satisfied.
Having forced the Arabs to cede Beirut they wanted
more and said so in no uncertain terms to Feisal. The
Emir was being strongly urged by certain of his

followers to resist, if necessary by force of arms, any demands that he accept French dominion and withdraw his forces from Syria. Unable to decide for himself what to do and uncertain how far he might be able to rely on British backing in an open conflict with France, Feisal sent an appeal to Lawrence, who immediately obtained from the British Government an invitation for him to come to London to discuss the position.

On 26th November the Emir landed at Marseilles from the British cruiser H.M.S. *Gloucester* accompanied by Nuri es Said. Lawrence was there to meet him, wearing his Arab dress. Meanwhile the French diplomatic cables had been humming between Paris, Jidda, Cairo and Damascus. A formal protest was made to Sherif Hussein that the French Government had not been properly informed of Feisal's mission —a futile gesture since the Emir was not taking orders from his father and was in any case on a mission to London and not to Paris. Then the hapless Bremond was dug out of some headquarters on the Western front and told to proceed immediately to meet Feisal and, while maintaining every reserve with him and his entourage, to extend to him the hospitality of France. As for Lawrence, Bremond's orders were to welcome him if he came dressed as a colonel but "not to accept him as an Arab"!

The Frenchman obeyed his pettifogging and pompous instructions to the letter and, on seeing Lawrence attending upon Feisal in his flowing white and gold robes, told the Emir of his government's views. Astonishingly enough, Feisal immediately ordered Lawrence to return to London and continued his conducted tour of France with Bremond, ending up in Paris with an official reception by President Poincaré and a lunch given in his honour at the Ministry of Foreign Affairs. Two weeks after he had landed in France, he left for Boulogne to find Lawrence once more awaiting him at the gang-plank of the ship that was to take him to England. Then, with Lawrence still faithfully in attendance, there followed a tour of Britain, a row of official visits and functions, an audience with King George V at which Lawrence, to the outraged horror of British officialdom, again wore Arab dress—and finally, a series of meetings at the Foreign Office to discuss his claims in Syria and to prepare for the Peace Conference which was about to open in Paris.

Lawrence's fidelity to Feisal during this period seems truly amazing after the rebuffs which he had received at the Emir's hands. Why, one may ask, should he have bothered with this ungrateful prince, who had shown him the door in Damascus? Why should he have gone on pleading for Feisal, after it had become clear that the Sherifian cause was torn apart by petty jealousies and intrigues and could never assert its claim to independence? Admittedly the British Cabinet had liked his plan for an Arab settlement. But, with every day that passed, the French were becoming more insistent upon their pound of flesh in Syria and French opinion was pressing for some compensation and reward in the Levant for French sufferings and losses on the Western front. It was scarcely possible that, with the Arabs weakened by their own divisions, the British would be able to hold to Lawrence's plan and let France have no more than Beirut and a strip of beach.

What then was it that drove Lawrence on so passionately? Undoubtedly it must have been his love for Syria, his first and his greatest love among the lands of Arabia, the "Garden of the Enchantress" where he had first found the beauty of the desert and washed his soul in its infinite purity, the place where he had made deep and lasting friendships with men, such as Sheikh Hamoudi, and found a kindred spirit in the beautiful young Arab, named Ahmed. Syria was what he had fought for, he now told himself— freedom and independence for Syria. Damascus had after all been in his dreams from that day three years before when he blurted out the name in the tense atmosphere of Feisal's camp at Hamra. His personal ambitions might lie in ruins, his services to the Emir might be unrewarded and his dreams of a free and united Arabia might be turning into a nightmare jigsaw puzzle of mandates, protectorates and colonies. But still he must fight to keep Syria out of the clutches of the French. By one of the many ironies of history Lawrence was destined to fail to save Syria but to succeed in saving Feisal.

26

Before the Paris Peace Conference opened in January 1919 Feisal and Lawrence were again in trouble with the French and with the Grand Sherif. The French at first refused to recognize the Emir as the representative of a state which they did not admit existed and which they were determined to use every artifice and pressure to ensure never would exist. The jealous old Sherif equally refused at the start of the conference to recognize his son as the representative of the Arab cause, still less of an Arab state, to which he had laid his own claims and whose throne he accused Feisal of usurping at the expense of his brother Abdulla. Only the British supported the lonely Emir and only with difficulty managed to persuade M. Clemenceau, the French Prime Minister aptly nicknamed "the Tiger," and the Grand Sherif to withdraw their objections.

It was an unhappy augury for the Arabs as the slim, white-robed figures of Feisal and Lawrence took their seats at the conference table amid the gilded splendours of the Salon de l'Horloge in the Quai d'Orsay. Erect, aloof and with the quiet distinction of the desert prince, the Emir faced the representatives of the nations that were to decide the future of his people and the fate of his cause. The French regarded him with barely concealed hostility. The Americans, on the other hand, led by President Wilson, felt a great sympathy towards this representative of a people oppressed by foreign domination. The author of the famous Fourteen Points, enshrining the principle of self-determination for all peoples, took a highly romanticized view of the Emir and his achievements. The British delegation, led by Mr. Lloyd George, found itself greatly embarrassed by the conflict of loyalties in which they found themselves placed.

❖   ❖   ❖

The British Government's embarrassments were a direct measure of the confusion of contradictory treaties, pledges and undertakings with which they and the entire conference were faced. First there was the British undertaking to the Grand Sherif in 1915 committing Britain to recognize Arab independence, if Hussein rebelled against the Turks. Second, there was the Sykes-Picot agreement of 1916 which provided for Arab states in Syria and Mesopotamia within French, British and Russian spheres of influence. The Russians had conveniently forfeited their rights in this respect by having a revolution and making a separate peace with Germany, but there was no sign of any weakening in the determination of the French to get their promised reward. The French claim to Syria, based partly on straight imperialism, partly on consideration of themselves as the historical protectors of the Christian faith and its adherents in the Arab world, was something that no French government could then abandon without dire political consequences. Third, there was the Balfour Declaration of 1917, pledging a National Home for the Jews in Palestine after the war. Fourth, there was the declaration of the British High Commissioner in Cairo in June 1918 "that the Arab zones liberated by the military action of their inhabitants would be entirely independent." Fifth, there was an Anglo-French declaration issued in November 1918 after the fall of Damascus which promised the Arabs of Syria and Mesopotamia "to show favour to indigenous governments and to guarantee the normal functioning without interference of the governments which the people themselves should elect." Over and above all this there were the Fourteen Points of Mr. Wilson, with the proclamation that the basis of future treaties should be the self-determination of peoples, a promise which had given rise to great hopes in the Arab world—as had been its clear intention.

How, one may ask, could so much confusion and contradiction have entered into the dealings of the British and Allied governments? Were the statesmen who made these pledges so double-faced that they cared only for expediency? Did they offer one thing to the Arabs to get them into the war and then agree the very opposite with the French to keep them fighting when the decimation of France's manhood threatened to take her out of the war? No, this is at once too simple and too heinous an answer. The real truth, so far as the British side is concerned, is that at least three different British policies were being carried on in the Middle East without any attempt at co-ordination and, so far as can be ascertained, without any real knowledge on the part of the authors of one as to what the others were doing and promising.

Sir Ronald Storrs in his *Orientations* makes this very clear. The Foreign Office in London were all for appeasing French susceptibilities and meeting French claims. Mr. Arthur Balfour, then Britain's Foreign Secretary, was also under strong Zionist pressures from Dr. Chaim Weizmann regarding the future of Palestine. For these reasons, the Foreign Office was responsible for the Sykes-Picot agreement and the Balfour Declaration. On the other hand, the British High Commission in Egypt—acting with the autonomy of the semi-sovereign government that it then was and anxious to help the British Commander-in-Chief to finish off the Turks as rapidly and effectively as possible—was promising independence to the Arabs in return for their co-operation in destroying the Ottoman empire. Then, cutting right across these two conflicting lines of policy, there was the Government of

India, another virtually autonomous British agency, which had its eyes on Mesopotamia as a vital link in the chain of imperial defence stretching from Britain through Gibraltar, Malta and Egypt to India and the Far East. The claims of New Delhi were strongly supported by the City of London, where longing glances were being cast in the direction of Mosul with its rich promise of abundant oil and copious revenues.

So much has been written about the broken British pledges to the Arabs and so much of Lawrence's post-war withdrawal from public affairs has been attributed to his sickness over Britain's alleged duplicity on this score that a brief look at the facts is not out of place at this point. The story begins in April 1914, when the Emir Abdulla visited Cairo for conversations with Lord Kitchener, then British High Commissioner in Egypt. The Turkish government in Constantinople, who by this time had come to distrust the Sherifian family and all its works, were incensed when they learned of Abdulla's visit and made representations to Kitchener not to receive the Emir. The High Commissioner complied with the request but instructed Storrs, then Oriental Secretary of the High Commission, to see Abdulla and find out what he wanted. The answer was "guns, for defence against the Turks." Storrs replied correctly that such a request could not possibly be entertained by a government in friendly relations with Turkey. Although the war clouds were gathering and trouble was already brewing between the Grand Sherif of Mecca and his Turkish masters, there was still a state of peace and Britain could not then properly involve herself in the internal conflicts of the Ottoman empire.

No more was said by either side until war broke out in August that same year. Thereafter the German propaganda campaign began with the object of bringing Turkey and her subject Arab peoples into the war against Britain and France. The Allies were described as the arch-enemies and Germany portrayed as the only European protector of Islam. The Turks, who bitterly resented Britain having taken their place in Egypt, became easy victims of this propaganda, especially when early Allied reverses promised the opportunity of an easy Turkish victory against the thinly held British line in Sinai. The German Kaiser was even prayed for in the mosques of Syria as Mohammed William or Hajji (Holy) Gilliom. Clearly it was only a matter of weeks before Turkey fell completely into the trap and joined with Germany in the so-called *jehad* (holy war) for which Berlin was calling.

With this in mind, Lord Kitchener, now Secretary of State for War in the British Cabinet, instructed Storrs in September 1914 from London to send an emissary to Abdulla to find out whether the Grand Sherif would stand with or against Britain, if Turkey should be coerced into the war at Germany's side. The reply was encouraging. Hussein and his sons and people would be on Britain's side and, in any case, did not believe that Germany would win. Lord Kitchener, acknowledging Hussein's answer on 31st October, pledged that "if the Arabs assist England in this war, England will guarantee that no intervention takes place in Arabia and will give the Arabs every assistance against external foreign aggression."

On 30th November 1914, Turkey entered the war against the Allies and ten days later Hussein sent a message to Cairo reaffirming his friendship to Britain but adding that he was not yet able to break with the Turks although he was awaiting a reasonable pretext to do so. No further word was said by either side until April 1915 when the Governor-General of the Sudan announced that Britain would guarantee in the peace settlement that the Arabian peninsula and the Holy places of Islam would be under an independent sovereign state. This pronouncement carefully refrained from any mention of boundaries and, three months later in July, the Sherif of Mecca sought to pin down his potential British ally and liberator. He proposed to Sir Henry McMahon, who had succeeded

Kitchener in Cairo, that Britain should recognize the right to independence of all the Arab areas of South-West Asia, excepting Aden, and should also acknowledge his claim to the Caliphate, which would have made him the "Pope" of Islam as well as King of Arabia. McMahon's reply was ambiguous in that he refused to commit the British government to a precise definition of areas, particularly in Western Syria and Lower Mesopotamia, and begged the question in respect of Hussein's other claims.

Nearly a year later, in May 1916, the Grand Sherif became alarmed by Turkey's connivance in German attempts to involve the Hejaz in the war and to establish radio stations on the Red Sea to open up communications with German forces in German East Africa. He despatched a message to Cairo asking Storrs to come urgently to the Hejaz to meet Abdulla and adding that "the movement will begin as soon as Feisal [then still a prisoner in Damascus] arrives at Mecca." Storrs arrived off Jidda on 5th June and conferred with the Sherif's sons, who informed him that hostilities had started that day with an attack on Medina by Feisal and Ali. Mecca would be attacked on 9th June. No politics were discussed and no further guarantees sought, save those of money and arms. Feisal and Ali were repulsed at Medina but, after four days of seige, Mecca surrendered on 13th June and Jidda three days later. Thereafter the revolt bogged down and might have petered out altogether amid mutual recriminations about lack of support between the Sherif and the British, had it not been for the drive and inspiration which Lawrence immediately began to impart to it after his self-appointed mission to Feisal.

Meanwhile, as Storrs tells us in *Orientations,* unknown to the British High Commission, the Sykes-Picot negotiations had resulted in an agreement for the tripartite carve-up of the Arab areas of the Ottoman empire into British, French and Russian spheres of influence, an agreement kept secret until it was divulged by the Bolsheviks after the 1917 revolution. At the same time the Government of India was in cahoots with Ibn Saud, the leader of the fanatical Wahhabi sect of Islam and a sworn enemy of the Hashemite family, and was busily making plans for colonizing Mesopotamia once the Turks had been driven out.

Had either or both of these rival policies been made known to McMahon at the time he could and—upright man that he was—probably would have either made it clear to Hussein that Britain would support none of his claims for Arab independence or have insisted, with the threat of resignation, that no conflicting pledges or undertakings be made by Britain to any third parties. As it was he was kept in the dark by a failure to co-ordinate policy between London, Cairo and New Delhi and, when the contradictions were finally exposed, he was removed from his post to spare him further embarrassment with the Arabs.

There is no doubt that the Arabs' belief, shared by Lawrence, that they were betrayed by Britain arises directly from the ambiguity of the High Commissioner's reply to Hussein's attempts to get the areas of independence precisely defined. Without clarification from London, which in the state of confusion over Middle East policy then prevailing was not forthcoming, he could only say which areas would not be independent—a vagueness which the Arabs justifiably took to mean that all areas not specifically defined (i.e. all but Western Syria and Lower Mesopotamia) would qualify for the independence which had been promised in general terms in the declarations of Lord Kitchener and the Governor-General of the Sudan. When these pronouncements were followed up by the Cairo declaration of June 1918 and the Anglo-French declaration of the following November, the Arabs were naturally convinced that the British would support them, however the French might seek to impose their rule upon liberated Arabia.

This certainly was Feisal's belief as the Peace Conference convened. As an opening bid he asserted the claim to independence of all Asian Arabia—the Hejaz, Nejd, Transjordan, Palestine, Syria and Mesopotamia—on the grounds that geographically and racially these areas were inseparable. He raised no difficulties about the Balfour Declaration and affirmed that he was all for Jewish immigration into Palestine, although opposed to the concept of a Jewish state on the same grounds of the inseparability of Palestine from the rest of the Arab world. "The Arabs and the Jews are cousins in race, have suffered similar oppressions . . . and by a happy concidence have been able to take the first step towards the attainment of their national ideals together," he wrote to Judge Felix Frankfurter from Paris in March 1919. "We will wish the Jews a most hearty welcome home . . . there is room in Syria for both of us."

One suspects that there was more of Lawrence than of Feisal in these magnanimous words. Lawrence had formed a great admiration for Chaim Weizmann since they met in Palestine after the fall of Jerusalem to discuss with the Emir the Zionist proposals for settling the Jews in the Holy Land, and he had always looked upon the Semitic race of Jews and Arabs as an indivisible whole. At the same time both he and Feisal no doubt felt that such avowed support for Zionism at this time would be good politics, in that it would still further commend the Arab cause to the American and British delegations by showing that an independent Arab state would not conflict with Jewish interests and claims as set forth in the Balfour Declaration. Unfortunately for them, and for subsequent history, their Palestine concession was not enough to secure independence for the Arabs, for it failed to reckon with French expansionism in Syria and the designs of India and of Western oil interests upon Mespotamia.

27

On 6th February 1919 Feisal appeared before the
Council of Ten to plead his case, Lawrence acting
as his adviser and interpreter. The Emir made the
most of the Arab contribution to the defeat of Turkey, exaggerating at times somewhat wildly the number of his warriors who had taken part and the casualties that they had suffered. But he was out of his
depth. Although born and reared amidst the intrigues
of the Orient, he was no match for the skilled and
determined diplomatists of the West who had already
virtually decided to throw him overboard. The British, while nominally supporting his claims for Syrian
independence, knew that they could not in the last
resort take Mesopotamia and forbid Syria to the
French. A further complication lay in the discovery
that, under the division of Arabia arranged in the
Sykes-Picot agreement, the oil wells of Mosul had
been placed in the area which was to be a French
zone of influence and authority. As might be expected, Clemenceau made the most of this trump
card to get a free hand in Syria; and, almost as
Feisal was making his first plea before the peace-
makers, British troops were giving way to French
throughout Western Syria. The utmost that might be
saved from the wreckage was the Syrian hinterland
and possibly Damascus.

Britain decided to settle for this and, as the conference dragged on through the spring of 1919, every
possible pressure was brought to bear on the French
to agree. All to no avail; Clemenceau knew the

strength of his position and doggedly insisted on a division of Syria into two zones, the coastal area to be a French colony and the hinterland a French protectorate. Lawrence fought desperately to defeat this plan, trying every artifice imaginable. He even used the occasion of a private audience with King George V—at which he was to be given his Order of the Bath—to arouse sympathy for Feisal's cause. Declining to receive any award from the sovereign head of a country which had made him a party to its betrayal of the Arabs, he left the King—to quote the monarch's own words—"holding the box in my hand." Back in Paris, Lawrence and Feisal went to see Colonel House, President Wilson's right-hand man, to urge that the American government should step in and set up an American mandate in Syria. Neither of these devices worked. The insult to King George boomeranged badly for Lawrence, causing more indignation than sympathy in Britain; and the furthest the American delegation would commit themselves was to suggest that an Allied commission of enquiry be sent to Syria—which proposition, due to lack of support by Britain and violent opposition by France, was transmuted into an all-American commission whose subsequent recommendation of a united Syria with Feisal as constitutional monarch was totally ignored.

Then came a further blow to Lawrence's efforts. Trouble broke out in Mesopotamia, with the tribes trying to resist by force the imposition of British rule by the Government of India. After the rebellion had been put down, the local British authorities discovered that the trouble-makers were financed out of moneys granted by Britain to the Sherif of Mecca and had been largely inspired by propaganda emanating from Damascus, where the Emir's well-meaning but immature young brother Zeid was deputizing for Feisal and finding himself no more capable of controlling the extremists in his entourage than his elder brother was of handling his so-called allies in Paris.

This could hardly have come at a worse moment for Feisal. Those powerful influences in the British Foreign Office, headed by Lord Curzon, who had all along been advocating a pro-French line at the expense of the Arabs, were now able to argue that loyalty to the Sherifian cause would not only alienate Britain's French ally, but would also play into the hands of the Arab extremists, who wanted to exclude all European and western influences and interests from the Arabian peninsula. From now on the final ditching of the Emir became a mere matter of time.

In May 1919, with still nothing decided about the fate of Syria, Feisal returned to Damascus to the cheers of his followers and the scowls of the French authorities. For Lawrence there were no cheers, as he returned to the home of his childhood in Oxford. His father had just died, two of his brothers had been killed in the war and his mother was girding herself to leave for China with his eldest brother, Bob, a medical missionary. Although his published letters tell little of his mood at that time, it is clear from his subsequent behaviour that the failure of his work in Paris, coming on top of the strains of moral torment, physical suffering and disappointed ambition during the war years, had brought him to the verge of a total breakdown. For hours on end he would sit in the same position, without moving, and with the same tortured expression on his face. After a while he could bear it no longer and decided to fly to Egypt to collect his papers and other belongings, which he had left behind in his hasty withdrawal from Damascus.

The aeroplane in which he travelled, a Handley-Page bomber, was in a shocking state of disrepair and crashed into a quarry attempting a forced landing in Italy, killing the two pilots. Although his own injuries included broken ribs and collar-bone, Lawrence climbed aboard yet another Handley-Page bomber and continued his journey to Cairo. Here he was met by anxious British officials who, acting on Foreign Office instructions, asked for an assurance that he was not planning to go on to Syria and make trouble for the French. News of his journey had come to the ears of the French government who had apparently taken quite seriously his joking threats in Paris—some of which he had made openly to Clemenceau and Marshal Foch—to take up arms against France rather than allow her to seize Syria.

A few weeks later Lawrence returned to Paris to make one last attempt to save his beloved Syria from French domination. But his efforts were again in vain. Feisal came to London to plead with Lloyd George and the British Cabinet but he was coldly told to make his peace with the French government. Britain had done all she could for him and was not prepared to upset her best friend in Europe for the sake of his throne. She was about to receive the Mesopotamian mandate and the Mosul oil concession and in return she had had to concede to France the mandate over all of Syria.

Lawrence had been excluded from these discussions with the Emir on the personal instructions of the British Prime Minister. Perhaps it was better for him that he was thus at least spared having to witness this final humiliation of Feisal. As it was he resorted to the traditional outlet of an Englishman's indignation, an angry letter to *The Times* of London, in which he reiterated point by point the arguments which he had been vainly stressing throughout the long months of the Paris Peace Conference. Less traditionally, though in an equally angry gesture, he attached the French Croix de Guerre with which Pisani had decorated him to the collar of Hogarth's dog and paraded it through the streets of Oxford.

❖   ❖   ❖

Feisal made his peace with Clemenceau and returned to Damascus on terms which made him little more than the head of a vassal state. In fact he would probably not have been allowed back in Syria at all, had it not been that the local French authorities were at that moment involved in putting down an attempt by some Turkish units, which had not yet been disbanded, to reimpose Ottoman rule in the frontier areas of Northern Syria. While they were so engaged, M. Georges Picot recommended that the less trouble they had with the Arabs the sooner the frontier disturbances could be settled and that to allow Feisal to return was for this purpose the lesser of two evils, for he would be more likely than anyone else to control the extremists in Damascus.

For several months Feisal played his part with dignity and restraint. Then in March 1920 the Arabs lost their patience and their tempers. Syria and Mesopotamia, or Iraq as it was about to be renamed, had been liberated from the Turks eighteen months before. Yet there was still no sign that the Arabs would be granted any real independence; they still had no king in either country; and their liberators were imposing their authority in a manner scarcely less offensive to Arab pride than that of the Turkish empire. An Arab congress met in Damascus and decided to assert their rights. Feisal was proclaimed King of Syria and his brother, Abdulla, King of Iraq.

France protested furiously at this act of defiance and invited Britain to join with her in annulling the proclamation. Curzon readily supported the French and the two powers jointly repudiated the decision of the congress. Feisal was peremptorily ordered to attend the San Remo Conference where all these matters were to be finally settled by France and Britain. The conference met the following month and, without further ado, awarded the Syrian mandate to France and the mandates over Iraq and Palestine to Britain. France renounced her claims to the Mosul oilfields and the area was ceded to Britain.

France had triumphed and Feisal's days were now numbered. It only required some pretext for the French authorities in Beirut to oust him altogether.

Georges Picot did not take long to find one. Early in July Britain was faced with a further outbreak of trouble among the tribes in the Euphrates valley and the extremists in Syria took their cue from their brothers in Iraq. French rail communications between Aleppo and their forces policing Northern Syria were threatened. General Gouraud, the French Commander-in-Chief and former commander in the French Sudan, renowned for his toughness in handling "native" problems, sent a brusque ultimatum to Feisal demanding the free use of these railways. As an earnest of France's determination Gouraud also gave orders for French troops to march on Damascus.

The Emir hesitated at first, believing that the British, and above all his friend Allenby, would never allow the French to get away with such high-handed treatment of their Arab allies. But such decisions no longer rested with Allenby. London had to be asked for instructions when Feisal's appeal for support was received in Cairo and London was at that time seriously perturbed and embarrassed by the outbreaks in Iraq. Thousands of British troops were involved and the cost of pacifying the country was more than £30,000,000 a year. How, it was asked in Whitehall, could Britain take the strongest action to deal with an insurrection affecting her own interests and oppose France in taking similar measures to safeguard her position? Besides, had it not been proved on the last occasion when trouble broke out in Iraq that it had been fomented in Damascus and financed by Mecca?

Allenby was told not to intervene and to let Feisal fight his own battles. The duty of conveying this bitter pill to the Emir fell to the unfortunate Kirkbride, who has related that Feisal behaved like a child when he received Britain's answer. Stunned by the news, he lost all dignity and alternately wept and cursed at his fate and the betrayal of his cause. When he had recovered his composure, the Emir made one last attempt to parley with the French, sending a telegram to General Gouraud in which he asked that the advance of French troops upon Damascus be halted to avoid bloodshed and to give time to discuss French demands. No reply came to this message, but the French advance continued and two days later Feisal capitulated completely. In a telegram making it plain that he personally would not fight, he accepted the French ultimatum in full and asked only that "the French army will retreat from the places it has just occupied." But, by this time, French blood was up and nothing was going to stop them taking Damascus and ousting Feisal from Syria. The surrender telegram was "lost" for four days to give time for French troops to reach the Syrian capital and defeat the Sherifian force that advanced to meet it. Then, on 27th July, the Emir received his notice to quit in a peremptory message which studiously avoided any mention of his acceptance of Gouraud's ultimatum and merely informed him that his train would leave for Palestine on the morning of the next day.

The news of Feisal's imminent departure spread around Damascus like a forest blaze and gave rise to riots and demonstrations by the Damascene population. The people who had risked their lives for their king during the Turkish occupation and had then saved him from the attempted *coup d'état* of Abd el Kader and the Druses were not going to accept a tame surrender of himself and them to the imperialist ambitions of yet another alien conqueror. In a last desperate effort, the Damascenes tried by sheer weight of numbers to bar the Emir's way out of the city. But Feisal had no further will to resist and ordered his Arab regulars under Nuri es Said to force a passage through the protesting populace. A few days later he arrived at Jerusalem, an erect but pathetic figure, fighting back the tears, and was granted refuge under British protection.

By a curious twist of history Feisal's humiliations

in Syria were, indirectly, to bring a far greater and more unexpected misfortune upon his father than upon himself. In a little over a year's time he was himself to be elected King of Iraq. But, within four years of Feisal's deposition in Syria, his father was to lose his throne in the Hejaz and to go into penurious exile with no compensations of any kind whatever.

The old Sherif had been so mortified by his son's acceptance of French terms on his return to Syria after the Peace Conference and so wounded by the alleged betrayal of the infidel's pledges to him that he decided to make a spectacular gesture to assert his independence and authority in the world of Islam. He proclaimed himself Caliph and "King of the Arab Lands." He could not have made a more unwise move. His old enemy, Ibn Saud of Nejd—the father of King Saud of Saudi Arabia—had for long been casting covetous glances at the Hejaz, regarding himself and his puritanical Wahhabi followers as the only fit and proper guardians of the Holy Cities of Islam—Mecca and Medina. Hussein's arrogant assertion gave him his pretext to set in motion a campaign of violence, propaganda and finally war against the Sherifian regime which ended in the incorporation of the Hejaz with the Nejd into the Kingdom of Saudi Arabia and in a Hashemite-Saudi feud which persists to this day like a blood-red thread through the tangled skein of Arab politics.

In July 1921, during the Cairo conference, Lawrence was sent to Jidda to try to persuade the Sherif to modify his claims and to stop antagonizing his neighbours. He was empowered to negotiate a treaty placing the Hejaz under British protection, if the old man could be brought to adopt a policy of conciliation. But the Sherif was not to be bought off by any British offers and, after a series of stormy meetings, broke off negotiations and shut himself away in Mecca, leaving Lawrence with no alternative but to return to Cairo. Still more unwisely Hussein ordered Abdulla to lead an expedition of four thousand men into the

Nejd to assert the authority of the new Caliph of Mecca. Abdulla's force was soon engaged by Wahhabi warriors and was all but annihilated in a terrible orgy of slaughter, Abdulla himself only narrowly escaping death or capture. The Sherif had stuck his neck out too far and Ibn Saud was not going to stop now until he had cleansed the Hejaz of the Hashemites and all who had dishonoured the name of Arabia by allying themselves with the infidels. By 1924 Hussein had abdicated and sought refuge in Cyprus, leaving his unfortunate and ailing eldest son, Ali, to defend the last remaining stronghold of Jidda against the victorious Wahhabis. Britain, although a generous financial supporter of the Sherif, refused to take sides in the conflict with Ibn Saud, so that, once the war supplies left over from the war had been exhausted, Jidda surrendered and Ali fled to Iraq where his brother Feisal provided him with a home in which to live out his life of exile.

The old Sherif had brought his troubles upon himself and there were few who wept over his final defeat. He had allowed his own suspicions, or those of his closest advisers, to dominate his actions and almost always his actions had been wrong and foolish. He had refused to help his son when he was carrying the burden of the Arab revolt upon his own slight shoulders; he had even intrigued against Feisal and incited mutiny among his soldiers, at the most crucial moment of the whole campaign: he had undermined his authority at the Peace Conference: and finally, when Feisal was trying to live with the meagre and uncertain results of his own labours in Paris, he had disowned him and declared his own independent authority as the Caliph and King of Arabia. That he should have finally been slapped down by a rival Arab chieftain, while the son whom he had sought to injure prospered in another kingdom, seems only poetic justice.

By a final act of irony, soon after his arrival in Cyprus, the old man was awarded by Britain the

Grand Cross of the Order of the Bath, the self-same order which Lawrence had refused to accept from his Sovereign in protest against Britain's betrayal of her pledges to the Sherif. Stranger still, he received it from the hands of Ronald Storrs, then Governor of Cyprus, who was Lawrence's henchman throughout the Arab Revolt and the principal purveyor of Britain's undertakings to the Arab movement.

28

After the collapse of all his dreams and the betrayal of all that he had fought for Lawrence probably wanted more than anything to crawl back into obscurity and forget the past. True, he had enjoyed the awed and curious glances that had been directed towards him as he accompanied Feisal on his daily rounds at the Paris Peace Conference. He had dressed himself in the white and gold robes of a Prince of Mecca to catch the eyes of the inquisitive and the admiring among the crowd and he had liked to know that he was being talked about as the "uncrowned king of Arabia." He would have had to be inhuman not to get some enjoyment out of such notoriety.

Yet his enjoyment was not by any means purely vanity. As often as not he was laughing at his ogling admirers as fools, misled by his aura of mystique. Also, while he scoffed at their gullibility, he could not in honesty refrain from despising himself for courting their stares and their compliments. His mission in Arabia had ended in betrayal and disaster and, however the "charlatan" that he admits existed in him craved for public esteem, the "genuine performer" deeply felt the performance to have been unworthy of his country and of himself. He had begun to write his own account of the Arab Revolt and of his part in it. The first draft of his epic *Seven Pillars of Wisdom* had been started in the feverish atmosphere of the Peace Conference and he was hoping as he returned to London at the end of 1919 to have a little peace and quiet to complete this great work.

But things did not work out that way. The reason was an America journalist named Lowell Thomas, the man who was destined to make Lawrence a legend throughout the English-speaking world. Thomas had been sent from America in 1917 as a war correspondent by a group of pro-Allied Americans who wanted to have good propaganda articles placed in the American press with a view to encouraging the United States to enter the war against Germany. Arriving in France he found nothing but seas of mud and scenes of slaughter scarcely suitable for his purpose. Somebody advised him to try the Middle East where at least it would be drier and possibly, with the Arab revolt and Allenby's campaign in full swing, more filled with spectacle and success. Thomas arrived in Palestine and soon afterwards was introduced to Lawrence by Ronald Storrs, then Governor of Jerusalem. This was just what he was looking for, a romantic British hero in a desert setting. Thomas let his imagination run riot, supplemented by a few interviews with his hero and a visit to Akaba to see Feisal's camp. Lawrence, amused by the whole business, posed often for Thomas's photographer in Arab dress and filled his eager ears with highly coloured accounts of his own rôle in the revolt and of the character and performance of the Bedouin.

Lowell Thomas accepted all of this and, after a brief visit to Petra, returned to the United States to write his articles. Then, when the war ended, he decided to gather all this material together and to organize a series of lectures in New York and across the United States. The lectures were illustrated with lantern slides and cinematographic film and entitled somewhat euphemistically, "With Allenby in Palestine and Lawrence in Arabia." Lawrence of course emerged as the shining white Crusader, a character without blemish, a hero pure, brave and honourable.

From his very first appearance at Madison Square Garden, Thomas was a huge success and Lawrence's name began to glitter across the pages of the American tabloids. This was a relatively uncynical age and the public liked their heroes straight, shining and without complexities or contradictions. One of his early performances was attended by an English impresario, Percy Burton, who, astonished that the American public should be learning of a British hero whose praises had not been sung at all in his own country, offered to put on Thomas's act in London, so that Britain might also hear of the greatness of this, her own son. Thomas jokingly retorted that he would come to London if Burton could guarantee the Royal Opera House as his auditorium and the King of England as his audience. A month later Burton cabled from London that both had been arranged.

From September 1919 to the beginning of 1920 Thomas performed at Covent Garden Opera House and the Albert Hall to an audience numbering over a million people and including Cabinet ministers, generals, admirals, ambassadors and the leaders of the business and social world of Britain. King George asked him for a private showing. From London he took himself to the British Commonwealth where he continued his astonishing lecture tour for the next four years. As for Lawrence, he became overnight a name to conjure with, a hero and a legend—a legend created by the man who, as he later admitted of himself, was in many respects completely misled by his hero.

This sudden acclaim aroused mixed feelings in Lawrence. Unable to resist the temptation to go and see himself eulogized, he would creep out from his modest bed-sitting-room and go to stand in the shadows at the back of the auditorium, while Lowell Thomas delivered his panegyric. Thomas states that he paid five or six such visits. Yet, after the first occasion Lawrence wrote to the American, "I saw your show last night. And thank God the lights were out!" A few days later, Thomas tells us, Lawrence went to see him and implored him to go back to America and to stop telling the public about his exploits. He said that he was being pursued by the press, by publishers and autograph-hunters and by ladies proposing marriage "whom he feared more than a Turkish army corps."

Later he spoke disparagingly about the man who had made him a legend, calling him "this wild American" who by turning him into "a matinée idol" had made his life a misery.

Nevertheless Lawrence seems to have shown no resentment at becoming, as a direct result of the Lowell Thomas lectures, the most photographed and painted figure in Britain at that time. On the contrary; he frequently visited the galleries where his portraits were being exhibited and posed in front of them for photographs. He found great enjoyment in the sudden notice which famous people like Lord Curzon took of him and readily seized every opportunity to cultivate men of letters, such as George Bernard Shaw, E. M. Forster, Thomas Hardy and Edward Garnett, and, in the world of the arts, Augustus John and Eric Kennington.

Which of these versions is one to believe gives the true reactions of Lawrence to the sudden popular acclaim that surrounded him? Or are they both true? There is no doubt that he liked, almost craved, public esteem and at the same time despised himself for seeking after it. He loved fame yet he was in some ways afraid of it. As Lowell Thomas remarked after Lawrence's death, quoting an old Turkish proverb, "he had a genius for backing into the limelight." Perhaps the craving for acclaim—which he describes so eloquently and tragically in his soul-searchings in the desert—was prompted by a determination to rise above his background of illegitimacy, and his fears by the feeling that had tormented him for so long that he was a fraud. In the desert he had wondered "if all established reputations were founded, like mine, on fraud." And here was his reputation being blazoned about the world in terms which set him on a par with Alexander and Napoleon and suggested that he had virtually destroyed the Ottoman empire single-handed.

At least one thing is certain. His sudden legendary status had helped his ego but it had not given him back his self-respect. Like the stimulant that gives the heart a temporary boost but leaves a hang-over effect after it has run its course, it flattered his vanity but left him ever more desperately needing to lose the shadow that had haunted him in and beyond Arabia.

29

By the summer of 1920 things had gone from bad to worse for the Arabs and especially for Feisal. Lawrence was deeply affected. Writing his book brought everything back in sharp relief and renewed his bitterness towards France and those Englishmen in authority whom he accused of betraying his Arab friends. For the past few months he had been living in Oxford where a fellowship of All Souls College had given him a brief cloistered peace to hide from the press and get on with his great memoir. But when Feisal went into exile Lawrence emerged from his hiding-place and, using his new status to the full, battered on the doors of the great men of Whitehall from Lloyd George downwards. For the most part his pleadings for the Arabs were greeted with a bored tolerance. But there was one notable exception— Winston Churchill, who was about to become Colonial Secretary and who had met Lawrence at the Paris Peace Conference and believed in him.

Churchill understood better than any of his Cabinet colleagues the causes that lay beneath the intense ferment which was then boiling up throughout the Middle East. For several years the Arab Bureau in Cairo had been sowing the wind of Arab nationalism to bring the Arabs to revolt against the Turks and Britain was now reaping the whirlwind of that same nationalism in Iraq. Britain could not expect the Arabs to draw a distinction between one type of alien rule and another and to accept calmly the substitution of British (or French) occupation for Turkish, after they had been inflamed by the war-cry of "Arabia for the Arabs." Everything was against this, as history had shown with the constant struggles of Islam against the infidels of Europe.

At the same time, to placate the pressures of Zionism, Britain had promised a national home for the Jewish people in Palestine. Although himself sympathetic to Zionism, Churchill understood that to carry such a policy through without a conflict with the Arabs of Palestine required the most careful and diplomatic handling. Curzon, whose department was then jointly with the India Office in charge of all these problems, was not the man for these tasks. An imperialist of the old school, he regarded Arab nationalism in the same way as the French. "Give 'em an inch and they'll take a mile." That type of attitude in Iraq was costing the British taxpayer annually well over three times what it had cost to destroy the Ottoman empire and, if not changed, would build up a legacy of hatred for Britain that might never be lived down.

Churchill persuaded Lloyd George to agree, upon his appointment as Colonial Secretary, to the transfer of responsibility for Middle East affairs to a new department of the Colonial Office which would be staffed with experts such as Clayton, Young and Meinertzhagen, Allenby's former assistant in Palestine. He also persuaded Lawrence to direct his energies and protests into positive channels by joining the department as Political Counsellor. At first Lawrence had refused to serve unless he could be assured in advance that Britain's pledges to the Arabs would be made good. After a compromise had been reached which permitted him considerable latitude in his job, Lawrence accepted Churchill's offer. J. B. Villars thinks that the arrival of Feisal in London at the end of 1920 probably hastened his decision, since "for Lawrence he constituted a living remorse."

Churchill's first action was to call a conference in Cairo in March 1921, which was attended by the newly appointed Governor of Iraq, Sir Percy Cox, Clayton, Cornwallis (a former member of the Arab Bureau and later to become British Ambassador in Baghdad), Young, Lord Trenchard, the founding father of the Royal Air Force, Gertrude Bell, the celebrated Orientalist, Jaafar Pasha, Feisal's former Chief of Staff, and Lawrence. The object of the conference was principally to decide how best to bring peace to Iraq. Some measure of autonomy had to be given to the government in Baghdad, while at the same time preserving a staging post in the chain of imperial defence and keeping control over those areas from which Britain derived her oil.

There was also the problem of Transjordan to be considered, the area of desert hills east of Palestine, criss-crossed by the comings and goings of the Arab revolt. Transjordan had been left out of the Paris and San Remo arrangements for its more important neighbours and, pending other dispositions, had been included in the British area of responsibility in Palestine. In January 1921 news had reached the British administration in Palestine that the Emir Abdulla had resigned as his father's Minister for Foreign Affairs in the Hejaz, had placed himself at the head of two thousand men and was marching on Damascus to expel the French and take over Syria as his own kingdom. To reach his goal he had to pass through Transjordan. Kirkbride, who was commissioner for this territory, asked for instructions from his superiors in Jerusalem. Should the Emir's advance be resisted? If so, he had a force of fifty policemen to take on the invaders! Or should Abdulla be welcomed to British territory? Jerusalem replied, somewhat unhelpfully, that it was most unlikely that the Emir would attempt such an invasion. Since his force was then at Maan, only a day's march away, Kirkbride took the law into his own hands and elected to give Abdulla the diplomatic treatment. Riding out to meet the Emir he bade him welcome on behalf of the British administration.

Abdulla, delighted and not a little surprised by his reception, thereupon called off the advance on Syria and, as the Cairo conference assembled, proclaimed himself Emir of Transjordan. One of the easier tasks of Churchill and his advisers was to accept this *fait accompli*. They made only two conditions—the first, that the Emir should recognize the validity of Britain's mandate in all of Palestine west of the Jordan river; the second, that he should renounce his avowed intention to invade and conquer Syria. Abdulla accepted both conditions without demur and the Transjordan question was duly settled. The first amends had been made to the Arabs.

As for Iraq, the conference favoured providing for a constitutional monarchy with Feisal as its monarch. He had already been sounded in England and, after a night of intensive discussions in Lord Winterton's country home in Sussex, had been persuaded by Lawrence to accept the throne, subject to the decision of a plebiscite. In June Feisal arrived in Iraq after an overwhelming vote of the people had elected him as their King. Sir Percy Cox became, by his own desire as well as by the decisions of the Cairo conference, an adviser instead of a controller, whose tact helped to smooth the passage of Feisal and paved the way for the transfer of power from British to Arab hands. The British army left Iraq and Britain's martial presence in the country was confined to the stationing of Air Force units in the Euphrates valley, an arrangement which was to persist, with only slight variations as to the status of the base, right up to the Iraq revolution of 1958.

The settlement of Iraq and the compensation which it gave to Feisal after his shabby humiliation in Syria owed much to the inspired teamwork of Lawrence and Churchill. In every way it typified their imaginative approach—a throne for Feisal, the progressive hand-over of power to the Arabs and the replacement of the army by the Air Force, the arm of the future, the modern guardian of Britain's overseas interests.

Even so, and making due allowance for pride of co-authorship, it is not a little surprising to learn from Lawrence's own pen that he regarded the decisions of the Cairo conference on Iraq and Transjordan as redemption in full by Britain of her promises to the Arabs. The claim was made in a manuscript preface, dated 18th November 1922, to an abridgment of the Oxford edition of the *Seven Pillars of Wisdom*, done by Edward Garnett but never published. The following is the relevant extract from the preface.

The book dates itself to 1919, when powerful elements in the British government were seeking to evade their wartime obligations to the Arabs. That stage ended in March 1921, when Mr. Winston Churchill took charge of the Middle East. He set honesty before expediency in order to fulfil our promises in the letter and in the spirit. He executed the whole McMahon undertaking (called a treaty by some who have not seen it) for Palestine, for Transjordan, and for Arabia. In Mesopotamia he went far beyond its provisions, giving to the Arabs more, and reserving for us much less, than Sir Henry McMahon had thought fit. In the affairs of French Syria he was not able to interfere and the Sherif of Mecca can fairly complain that the settlement there is not yet in accordance with the Anglo-French agreement of 1916, or with our word to him. I say "not yet" advisedly, since the McMahon proposals were likely to have imposed themselves eventually, even if Mr. Churchill's progressive British military withdrawal from Mesopotamia had not come to prejudge the future of all the Arab areas. I do not wish to publish secret documents, nor to make long explanations; but must put on record my conviction that England is out of the Arab affair with clean hands.

Lawrence made a similar assertion in one of his rare footnotes in the text of the *Seven Pillars*, though he there added remorsefully that Britain's acquittal with clean hands had come "three years too late to earn the gratitude which peoples, if not states, can pay." He also told his biographer, Robert Graves, that the Cairo settlement "should weigh more than the fighting."

It is impossible to say how far these affirmations reflected a genuine belief in the results of his work in Cairo or how much was designed to provide him with a pretext to escape from further responsibilities in Arabia. Liddell Hart believes that he really felt his mission had been redeemed and his pledges fulfilled. But this is a little difficult to accept. For one thing the settlement, while compensating Feisal for the loss of Syria, did nothing—and at this late stage could do nothing—to compensate Syria for the loss of Feisal. Lawrence's optimistic reflection that Churchill's liberal policy in Iraq would "prejudge the future of all the Arab areas" was sadly disproved by events. Syria did not gain her freedom until nearly twenty-five years later; and, if we are to believe his earlier protestations in London, Paris and Damascus, Syria counted for infinitely more in his eyes than all the rest of Arabia put together.

If he had really felt so gratified by the results of the Cairo conference, why was he not content to settle down in the post of Chief British Representative in Transjordan to which Churchill appointed him in the summer of 1921? True he had never got on with Abdulla and probably liked even less having to intervene to stop his agents stirring up trouble in the Jebel Druse borderlands of Syria. In the frequent skirmishes between the French and Abdulla's Arabs which were taking place when he took up his post, his heart must clearly have been with the Arabs. But, as Churchill records, "he used his plenary powers with his old vigour, he removed officers, he used force, he restored complete tranquillity." (Certain French writers have claimed that Lawrence made more trouble for the French in Syria than he prevented at that time, but a closer reading of history suggests that there was enough trouble brewing in Syria as a result of French handling of the Arabs not to require any incitement from outside.)

Still Lawrence felt that he could not stay in Arabia and by the end of the year he left for England never to return. Two months later, having completed a year of service with the Colonial office, he asked to be released. Churchill, like Allenby in Damascus, pressed him to stay. Unlike Allenby, he persuaded Lawrence to soldier on for five months, but in June he received a peremptory announcement that his strange young adviser could wait no longer. Churchill, commenting on his brief but momentous association with Lawrence, said, "He is a fine animal, but he cannot live in captivity." On another occasion he remarked, "The wonder was that he was able to sink his personality, to bend his imperious will, and pool his knowledge in the common stock." Yet less than two months later Lawrence had joined the Royal Air Force as an aircraftman second class, voluntarily submitting himself to captivity, changing his famous name and sinking his personality to the lowest rank in the British armed forces.

30

The story of Lawrence's classic memoir, the *Seven Pillars of Wisdom,* could be a book in itself. He began writing it during the Paris Peace Conference early in 1919 and had almost finished when in November of the same year he lost four-fifths of the manuscript, while changing trains at Reading station on his way home from London to Oxford. Undaunted by this disaster, he set to work again, locked himself up in the attic of a friend's house in Barton Street, Westminster, and in a superhuman burst of activity completed his second draft by the end of 1920.

The effort took a tremendous toll of his strength. Night and day he applied himself to his task—on one occasion for forty-eight hours at a stretch—re-living the drama of his war-time campaigns, the nightmarish experiences of his life in the desert and the soul-destroying sensations of hypocrisy and fraudulent dealings between his British masters and his Arab friends. During this time he lived almost entirely off his supply of nervous energy, ate next to nothing and saw practically nobody. By the time he had finished he was at the point of total exhaustion. Liddell Hart states from his own personal observation of Lawrence that "it was the exaltation of writing the *Seven Pillars of Wisdom* even more than the strain of war that brought him perilously close to the border line."

Yet still Lawrence was not satisfied with the result, which ran to over 400,000 words and was, in his view, "careless in style and hopelessly bad as a text."

He took the manuscript with him after he had joined Churchill's Colonial Office team on his journeys to Egypt, the Hejaz and Transjordan. There he revised and rewrote the whole work, reducing it to some 330,000 words. On completing the revision by the middle of 1922, he sent it to the Oxford Times to print in linotype, like the Holy Bible. Eight copies were so printed, five of which were bound and sent by Lawrence for comments and criticisms to friends of his from the war, such as Buxton, Dawnay and Bartholomew, and to artists and writers of more recent acquaintance, including Eric Kennington, George Bernard Shaw, Edward Garnett and Robert Graves.

Lawrence approached these literary figures with more than ordinary modesty, apologizing to Shaw especially for troubling him with the request that he read and comment upon such a long work. "Suddenly I remembered," he wrote to Shaw, "that your time was rubies and that if you spent hours over it I might be preventing, and would surely be delaying, another Caesar or Heartbreak. . . . Please don't, out of kindness, bore yourself. It's more like the heaps of stone-chips left in the quarry after the builders had finished, than like the great pyramid itself. . . ."

Bernard Shaw had indeed been reluctant to read the *Seven Pillars of Wisdom* and was only with difficulty persuaded to do so by his wife, Charlotte, after she had herself read it and pronounced it a masterpiece. But the famous playwright was constrained in the end to agree with Mrs. Shaw's opinion and, together with Edward Garnett and other friends, went to work to try and persuade the author to publish his epic. In spite of this encouragement and praise, Lawrence was nevertheless in two minds on the question of publication. He wrote to Edward Garnett from his R.A.F. station at Uxbridge, "I decided yesterday in Church (Church-parade!) that I ought to publish nothing. Today I feel inclined to publish. Am I neurasthenic or just feeble-willed?"

His hesitations were probably due not only to a fear

of unfavourable criticism and unfriendly reviews but also to a reluctance to publish something so personal as those tormented chapters where he searched his soul and discovered that "the truth was I did not like the 'myself' I could see and hear." It was one thing to write down for a few friends to read everything that he had done and seen and felt during the desert war exactly as he had remembered these experiences; it was quite another to publish all this to the world and so to stand naked before the gaze of all mankind. As for rewriting it all yet again or revising the book so as to leave out the personal chapters, Lawrence then claimed that he had neither the time to tackle the job nor the inclination to publish something that was not a full and complete account of his experiences.

It appears, however, that he later relented and reached an agreement with Jonathan Cape to publish an abridgment which Edward Garnett had prepared for him. But the contract reached him on or very shortly before the day at the beginning of 1923 when the press discovered that the John Hume Ross in the ranks of the Royal Air Force was Colonel T. E. Lawrence, which revelation promptly led to his dismissal from the service. Writing to Bernard Shaw shortly afterwards Lawrence said that when "the first foul shout about me came in the Daily Express I cancelled (or rather I refused to complete and sign) the contract with Cape for publishing an abridgment. Cape was furious. . . ." Lawrence went on to say:

A while later I was sorry to have cancelled it, and I began to think of publishing, not an abridgment, but the whole story, as you have advised. So I sketched to Cape the possibility of a limited, privately printed, subscription edition of 2000 copies. . . . Cape was staggered for the first moment, but then rose to it. . . . It took the form of a beautiful contract, sent to me to sign: and that very day I got my dismissal from the Air Ministry, and so I've cancelled it too.

Shaw's paeans of praise appear to have had some effect in convincing Lawrence that he had compiled a great book. In June 1923 he wrote to his old friend Hogarth, "When I joined the RAF . . . I thought my Arab Revolt book very bad. Since then Shaw has turned my mind slowly to consider it good: and there's another ambition gone, for it was always my hope to write a decent book. . . ." Yet at other times he took the opposite view, writing to Edward Garnett describing his work as "irredeemable, irremediable muck," which deepened his "gloomy view" of it every time he waded through it. "If you want to see how good situations, good characters, good material can be wickedly bungled, refer to any page, passim. There isn't a scribbler in Fleet Street who wouldn't have got more fire and colour into every paragraph. How on earth can you have thought it passable."

Even allowing that such self-depreciation was so much false modesty, it is not clear exactly why Lawrence was finally prompted to revert to the idea of a privately printed subscription edition. It has been said that, when Gertrude Bell asked to be lent a copy of the Oxford edition and had to be refused because all available copies were already out on loan, he decided to have another edition printed for his friends. More likely, Lawrence was torn between the desire to see himself in print and the fear of the critics tearing his work to pieces—the old craving for fame battling once again with the dread of being exposed as a failure. Whatever the reason, he eventually decided to compromise and to have a hundred copies printed of a subscription edition to be sold for thirty guineas each. But the showman in him demanded that each copy be printed in the finest style possible and illustrated by some of the best artists, including Augustus John and Eric Kennington, whom he had commissioned to paint and sketch himself, Feisal, Allenby and more than a score of other British and Arab personalities associated with the Arab Revolt. Once again he set to work to revise and rewrite the book, eliminating certain references to senior British officers which he jokingly told Kennington would have landed him in at least twenty-seven libel actions had they been published. Certain personal passages that appeared in the Oxford edition were also redrafted or dropped altogether and the whole text was tightened up and shortened by some fifteen per cent. But in all his life he never relented from his decision not to publish the *Seven Pillars of Wisdom,* and it was left to his youngest brother, Arnold Lawrence, as his literary heir, to make this masterpiece available to the public after his death in 1935.

The work of revision took him until 1925, and the following year the subscribers' edition of the *Seven Pillars of Wisdom* appeared. Its success was immediate and far beyond the dreams (or fears?) of its author. Demand for it was so great and the supply so limited that some of the copies, originally bought for thirty guineas, were resold for five and six hundred pounds and people were offering in the advertisement columns of the press five pounds a week for the loan of one copy. But none of these fantastic profits went into the pockets of the author or his publishers, Jonathan Cape, and such was the lavishness with which the book had been produced and so great the cost of illustrating it that the project incurred a heavy financial loss. To meet this deficit, Cape persuaded Lawrence to publish an abridged edition—to be called *Revolt in the Desert*—with most of the personal reflections and self-analysis deleted. Lawrence made only one stipulation—that the book should not be published until he was out of the country. Cape agreed: in December 1926 Lawrence left for a Royal Air Force station in India and a few weeks later *Revolt in the Desert* reached the booksellers. Its success was also immediate and the profits not only paid off the cost of the *Seven Pillars of Wisdom* but left a net gain of £15,000. Typical of a man who neither understood nor cared for money, Lawrence then withdrew the book from circulation and, refusing to benefit from a best-seller written in British and Arab blood, gave the whole of his share in the profits to service charities.

This story of the conception and birth of the *Seven Pillars of Wisdom* is as characteristic of Lawrence as any other single episode of his life. It symbolizes all the contradictions of his personality and all the hopes and fears, the determination of the will and neurosis of the mind that went to make up his extraordinary character. First, there was the absolute resolve to write the book at no matter what cost in mental and physical strain. Accompanying this was the showman's desire to achieve a first-class production in terms of writing and illustration. Then, once the task was accomplished, came the desperate fear to submit his product to public scrutiny, even though such experienced critics as Shaw and Garnett assured him of a spectacular success. Finally, when the success had been achieved, there came the refusal to profit by it.

❖   ❖   ❖

Every book has its critics and every author his detractors. But, whatever else may be said about the *Seven Pillars of Wisdom,* it is and will remain an epic and a classic. J. B. Villars says of it:

> The profundity of the introspection and the nakedness of the confessions make one think of Rousseau or rather of Proust or Gide. Though a book on war it contributes to our researches into the obscurities of the human heart. In the course of a painful quest into a rent and complex self, and behind a screen of dignity and gravity can be perceived some very dangerous problems; few authors have described the troubled twistings of the serpent with so much penetration and sincerity.

Besides, as Villars also points out, Lawrence's

memoir blazed a new trail in writing and proved to be the forerunner of Malraux, Koestler and Jean-Paul Sartre. Today the reading public is accustomed to books that tell of atrocities, of treachery and of the brutality and futility of war. But, when Lawrence wrote the *Seven Pillars of Wisdom,* he was breaking new ground. Not content to raise just a corner of the curtain that had hitherto concealed the real horrors of modern war from the public gaze, he swept it aside and exposed in all its nakedness the truth of the desert campaign as he had seen it and lived through it, sparing neither himself nor his associates in the telling.

Of course his detractors, such as Richard Aldington, have found amidst the not unnumerous contradictions in the text and in Lawrence's own personal conclusions evidence to declare the whole work a monstrous lie. Lawrence must bear a little of the blame for this himself. For one thing he appears to have made several contradictory assertions about the contents of the book. In the first introduction that he wrote for his memoir—revealed in a later work published by his brother Professor Arnold Lawrence and entitled *Oriental Assembly*—he said, "It seemed to me historically needful to reproduce the tale, as perhaps no one but myself in Feisal's army had thought of writing down at the time what we felt, what we hoped, what we tried." But he finished on a contradictory note. "I began in my reports to conceal the true stories of things and to persuade the few Arabs who knew to an equal reticence. In this book also, for the last time I mean to be my own judge on what to say." Again to Colonel Meinertzhagen, a former staff officer with General Allenby, he gave the impression that his book was based on falsehoods but that having become a legendary hero he had had to live up to the legend.

Yet for all of this none of those most closely associated with his part in the Arab revolt uttered a word of denial or contradiction of his account. Allenby, Clayton, Storrs, Newcombe, Joyce, Young and

Dawnay, all of them were sent the work in its original form and not one of them quarrelled with it. Such tacit acquiescence offers a convincing guarantee of authenticity, which all the bitter sarcasm of an Aldington cannot shatter.

There is no doubt that Lawrence left out certain facts and happenings which did not tie in with his conclusions. For one thing, he made little mention of the British and even less of the French contribution to the winning of the war against Turkey and to the success of the Arab revolt. As a result of this exercise of his prejudice against the French, the unwitting reader is left with the impression that the Arabs received little Allied help save some gold and a few guns supplied by Britain at Lawrence's request. Also his failure to analyse the precise extent of Britain's political commitments and promises to Sherif Hussein suggests that far more was offered and subsequently denied to the Arabs than was the case. It is fair to say that Lawrence should have acknowledged these facts even though he may not have realized at the time of writing that his book was destined to become a classic.

But Lawrence was writing subjectively of the Arab revolt and "of me in it," not objectively about the Middle East campaign as a whole. He was not merely setting down a record of events but was also pleading a cause. His remark to Meinertzhagen was more likely intended to convey his overwhelming revulsion at being lauded as a hero, when throughout the desert campaign all that he had felt was a fake, than to suggest that he was filling his book with false tales of his own heroism. (In fact his confessions of fear and fraudulence are far more numerous and impressive than any of the tales of his heroics.) As for the contradictions in his conclusions, far from showing Lawrence to be a liar, they more likely reflected his essential truthfulness, in that he was clearly determined to set down his thoughts and observations as they occurred to him at the time that they occurred to him, regardless of how they may have changed a few chapters later. Better to record the truth as he saw it down the years of war than to suppress or modify it to fit the passage of time.

Besides, Lawrence was himself a mass of contradictions and his life conformed to his kaleidoscopic pattern. Why then should he be called a liar, because his own memoir reflected his own character and existence? As J. B. Villars remarks:

> All art is founded on truth. Transposed and modified it remains the point on which the artist and the human touch. It is the points of truth which constitute, amidst themes that are imaginary, the strength of masterpieces. Lawrence was too much an artist to escape from this law. He always ends, having tried to hide everything, by revealing the truth, and almost all his lies are contradicted by parallel confessions. His most exalted heroes, the Arabs, Feisal, and even his own person, he manages to depict as he really saw, with his cruel clearness of insight. And this is why the *Seven Pillars* appears to have been written beneath the sign of contradiction.

Lawrence's epic showed him to be as keen to confess himself as to plead his cause, to demonstrate his own frailties and littleness against the vast and lurid backcloth of the history that he helped to make. True, the reader of the *Seven Pillars of Wisdom* will find a quality in the style altogether different from the pedestrian rapportage of the more ordinary chroniclers of war. In places he will come across purple passages that seem to have been worked on with the meticulous care of a sculptor. Then a few sentences later the whole magnificent portrait will be besmirched by some grotesque caricature. Equally there are passages moving beyond description in the simplicity of language and the infinite understanding and compassion that they show for the failings of human beings under terrible strain. But the fact that Lawrence could, and did, write of his war with such colour and consummate artistry does not make his book a work of fiction. Rather does it mean that he had the perception and understanding to see deep into the hearts of his battle comrades, the courage to set down everything that he saw and that rare gift of language that can transform the printed page into a living stage.

In the course of writing the second draft of his memoir, Lawrence confessed that "I had had one craving all my life—for the power of self-expression in some imaginative form." He certainly found it in the *Seven Pillars of Wisdom*. As Sir Winston Churchill wrote in his own commentary on this classic of the English language, "There are no mass effects. All is intense, individual, sentient—and yet cast in conditions which seem to forbid human existence. Through all, one mind, one soul, one willpower. An epic, a prodigy, a tale of torment, and in the heart of it—a Man."

31

✦✦✦✦✦✦✦✦✦✦✦✦✦✦ *REDUCED TO THE RANKS*

Before enlisting in the Royal Air Force, Lawrence took the name of John Hume Ross. The change, although not legally effected as was his later adoption of the name of Shaw, served the dual purpose of making a complete break with his past as Colonel T. E. Lawrence and of reducing him to an obscurity necessary for him to enlist in a service which, as later events were to prove, did not take to the idea of having a legendary figure in its ranks.

Beside his desire to forget the war, the Cairo conference had, in Lawrence's view, brought his work in the Middle East to an end. Feisal was securely installed in Iraq and Abdulla in Transjordan and, although Abdulla's friends failed to share Lawrence's view of the Cairo decisions which they bitterly criticized as trampling underfoot the liberties of the Arabs, he was no longer prepared to stay and argue with them. There was nothing to be done about Syria, where the French were impregnably situated and were not going to be moved by the rumblings and grumblings in Amman. As for Sherif Hussein, he was riding irresistibly towards his own doom and nobody could stop him. Having learnt the bitter lesson that kings like kingmakers out of the way once their job is completed, Lawrence knew that there was nothing more for him to do in Arabia. Churchill had offered him a governorship but he had refused. For better or worse, he felt that the Arabs must get on with the job of learning to govern themselves and the rôle of a gold-braided bystander had no appeal for him. His tortured mind cried out for an altogether simpler and more constructive task.

The mental strain of the past six years had brought him to the verge of a breakdown. Only by completely severing all his links with the past could he find the cure for his neurosis, which he felt he needed desperately, if he was to retain his sanity. He had often spoken of the possibility of enlisting in one of the services and had discussed with Leopold Amery, a Conservative M.P. and friend of Churchill's, the prospect of secluding himself as a coastguard or lighthouse keeper. He had at the same time frequently discussed the question of his sanity with friends, writing, for example, as he did to Lionel Curtis, "sometimes I wonder how far mad I am and if a madhouse would not be my next (and merciful) stage." Less tactfully, he also replied when the recruiting officer asked why he wished to enlist in the R.A.F., "I think I must have had a mental breakdown, Sir." This mania for losing his shadow was also reflected in his entries in *Who's Who* over the years 1922–1935. At the outset he listed against his name all his wartime assignments and decorations, but progressively shed them over the later years until virtually none of the war story remained and he appeared simply as a scholar and archaeologist.

It has been said by some observers that his principal reason for enlistment was to seek notoriety, and that, by ostentatiously disappearing under an assumed name and so surrounding himself with an aura of mystery, he would draw to himself a far greater attention from the press than by continuing to live at All Souls, Oxford, under his own name or by accepting some post of distinction overseas in the service of his country. The theory is just a little too subtle to ring true. He did not, it is true, conceal his real identity from all his friends. Shaw and Garnett were among those who were in the secret. But a secret it was to the outside world and there can be little doubt of Lawrence's extreme dismay when he was given away by an officer at his station at Uxbridge and dismissed from the R.A.F. when the story broke under banner headlines in the popular press.

Lawrence himself gave three reasons for taking the remarkable step of enlisting in the ranks of the Air Force. First, security; second, escape from responsibility; and third, self-degradation. To his old friend Hogarth he wrote in answer to the question why he had enlisted, "The security of it first; seven years existence guaranteed—I haven't any longer the mind to fight for sustenance. As you realise I've finished with the 'Lawrence' episode. I don't like what rumour makes of him . . . and the life of politics wearied me out, by worrying me overmuch." To Lionel Curtis he said, "You know I joined partly to make myself unemployable, or rather impossible in my old trade." And in another letter:

> Seven years of this will make me impossible for anyone to suggest for a responsible position, and that self-degradation is my aim. I haven't the impulse and the conviction to fit what I know to be my power of moulding men and things. . . . I have to answer here only for my cleanness of skin, cleanness of clothes, and a certain mechanical neatness of physical evolution upon the barrack square. There has not been presented to me, since I have been here, a single choice: everything is ordained . . . in determinism complete there lies the perfect peace I have so longed for. Free will I've tried, and rejected; authority I've rejected . . . action I've rejected: and the intellectual life. . . . They were all failures, and my reason tells me therefore that obedience, nescience, will also fail . . . and yet in spite of reason I am trying it.

To those who, like Young, on the eve of Lawrence's enlistment urged him at least to take a commission, he replied that he did not think much of the officers or the orders in the R.A.F. Nothing would persuade him to become a mere purveyor of stupid orders. He had either to be at the top where he could ensure that foolish orders were not handed down or at the bottom where obedience would close his eyes to their stupidity: and, because he had had enough of responsibility and had "rejected authority," he preferred to be at the bottom.

On 30th August 1922 John Hume Ross entered the R.A.F. recruiting office in Henrietta Street, London, after two hours pacing up and down the street, trembling like a leaf in anticipation of the reception that awaited him beyond the door with the posters inviting the young men of England to join in the conquest of the air. It was not long before his fears seemed to be confirmed. The identification papers that he presented to the presiding officer were a clumsy forgery and aroused immediate suspicion that he was an ex-convict, a suspicion which was strengthened when, after he had stripped for medical examination, his back revealed the marks of severe flogging. He tried to brazen it out with talk of having torn himself on a barbed wire fence, but to no avail. He was told he was not wanted. But after seeking the personal intervention of Air Marshal Lord Trenchard, the R.A.F.'s founder, and of the Secretary of State for Air, who overruled the recruiting officers, Lawrence (alias Ross) squeaked his way into the Air Force and presented himself for initial training at the Uxbridge depot. His contract of service was an unusual one, Trenchard having made it clear to him that it could be terminated at a month's notice by either party. The Air Marshal, although taken by Lawrence's statement that "the conquest of the last element, the air, seems to me the only major task of our generation," had only with difficulty been persuaded to become a party to this extraordinary project, fearing that, if the recruit's true identity were discovered, it would be embarrassing for his superiors and bad for discipline.

Lawrence's early experiences at Uxbridge were far from what he had hoped. During the war he had found a comradeship with the ordinary private soldier far easier than anything that he had known with his equals or superiors in rank. He had hoped to rediscover this comradeship in the R.A.F. but instead he found himself a fish out of water, surrounded by a coarse, licentious and rowdy soldiery, whose language and habits he could neither understand nor imitate, and ordered about by non-commissioned officers whose principal method of discipline was a constant verbal flagellation of everybody inferior to them, and especially the new recruits. For a sensitive intellectual searching for peace and security away from the strident world outside, this never ceasing noise and the sour-scented vulgarity of the barrack room was a veritable nightmare. "Our hut-refuge was become libertine, brutal, loud-voiced, unwashed," he wrote in his diary, later to be published under the title *The Mint*.

After two months at Uxbridge Lawrence was sent to the R.A.F. station at Farnborough, a flying-training and photographic instruction centre. Although not permitted to fly he found here some congenial tasks, busying himself with aeroplane engines and in the photographic laboratory. But, just as he was beginning to find his new self and to lose the shadow of "Lawrence of Arabia," he was given away to the press. On 27th December 1922 the front and centre pages of the *Daily Express* announced to the world that the fabulous and legendary eccentric, Colonel Lawrence, was masquerading in the ranks of the Royal Air Force as Aircraftman Ross. Immediately, the Farnborough camp was besieged with press reporters and photographers demanding interviews and pictures of Lawrence. The Air Force authorities considered the situation impossible and a month later he was dismissed from the service in accordance with the contract laid down by Trenchard.

For several weeks he badgered his friends in high places, and Trenchard in particular, to help him to re-enlist in the R.A.F. But, although his conduct sheet had no black marks, he had in his subtle and impish way not been able to resist making many of his immediate superiors at Uxbridge feel foolish and intellectually inferior to him and his wheedlings proved unavailing in removing the fear of the authorities that his presence in the ranks would be "bad for discipline." The most that Trenchard would undertake was to reconsider his application if he obtained a good character after a period of service in the army. Alternatively, he could have a commission in the R.A.F. right away.

Lawrence stuck to his guns, refused the commission and, early in March 1923, joined the Tank Corps after changing his name a second time to T. E. Shaw. He was sent to the tank training camp at Bovington in Dorset. After completing his drill training he was assigned to the quartermaster's store where his job was to mark and fit army clothing. The comparative peace and quiet of this task gave him time to devote to his writing. It was here that he completed his revision of the Oxford edition of the *Seven Pillars of Wisdom*. Also, to earn a little spare cash, he translated a couple of French novels into English for Jonathan Cape.

Lawrence was also able to indulge another of his passions—speed. Through personal contact with George Brough, the manufacturer of the motorcycle which bears his name, Lawrence was able every year to obtain at a much reduced price a machine that had been used for demonstration purposes. From then on the Brough motor-cycle became his only means of locomotion on land. He spurned motor cars as insensate things only of use in wet weather. "Speed," he explained to Liddell Hart, "is the second oldest animal craving in our nature." Lawrence certainly indulged the craving—the only heritage from his desert campaign that he did not seek to cast away. Dropping in on old friends, such as Bernard Shaw, Kennington and Thomas Hardy, he averaged between four and six hundred miles a week and rode at speeds of eighty to one hundred miles per hour wherever the going permitted.

By way of contrast, he also found next to Bovington camp the only home that he ever owned—a derelict cottage, called Clouds Hill, which he rebuilt and furnished with a bed, three chairs, a hundred books and a gramophone to gratify his pleasure in music. The cottage became his principal interest outside his work and he would describe in minute detail the improvements and additions he was carrying out in every letter that he wrote to his mother from now on. It became his permanent headquarters for entertaining his friends. Such entertainment was in his case more intellectual than gastronomic. Owing to a phobia that he had for the smell of cooking, the food that he gave his guests was always tinned and was usually eaten straight from the tin to save washing up. Tea was the only thing he permitted in the way of cooking and Mrs. Eric Kennington recalls that his method of washing up after tea was to set the crocks on the stepped path in the garden, to pour boiling water onto the top step and to let it flow down from one to another!

After a year's service in the Tank Corps, Lawrence let it be known to Trenchard that he had, in his own view, fulfilled the conditions of his re-enlistment in the Air Force. In spite of the relative peace and quiet of life at Bovington, he was not happy and could only think of getting back to the service of his choice. He found difficulty in keeping up with men much younger and fitter than himself at the strenuous physical training that was part of the routine. On this account he was continually nagged by his neurotic fears of failing to live up to his fellow men. Writing to Hogarth he said:

It will be a puzzle for my biographer (if I have one of those unprofitable things) to reconcile my joy in the R.A.F. with my disgust with the Army. The R.A.F. is utterly unlike this place: the men are so different and their hopes and minds and talk. . . . I feel queerly homesick whenever I see a blue uniform in the street. But for going back to the R.A.F.—there my hands are tied. Trenchard . . . couldn't do it: asked me to take my discharge as final: and he's not a mind-changer. . . .

Trenchard had indeed set himself against Lawrence returning to the Air Force, for a year later in May 1925 he made it clear in reply to a further appeal from Lawrence that the application had been turned down once more. Lawrence's hopes had earlier been raised by a request from the Labour Secretary of State for Air, Lord Thomson, that he should write an official history of the R.A.F. He had agreed, provided that he should be allowed to re-enlist when the work was completed. Lord Thomson had however refused to accept this condition and the proposal was withdrawn.

Lawrence then tried another tack. He had recently met John Buchan, the famous author and novelist who later became Lord Tweedsmuir and Governor-General of Canada. Buchan was on terms of close friendship with Stanley Baldwin, who had just been re-elected Prime Minister after the defeat of the Labour government in the 1924 election. He was also a friend of Edward Garnett. Lawrence appealed to Buchan to intercede on his behalf and at the same time wrote to Garnett saying, "I'm no bloody good on earth. So I'm going to quit: but in my usual comic fashion. I'm going to finish the reprint and square up with Cape before I hop it. . . . I shall bequeath you my notes on life in the R.A.F." The thinly veiled threat of suicide did the trick. Garnett was alarmed and wrote immediately to Buchan and Shaw, who asked Baldwin to intervene with the R.A.F. authorities, if only to avoid a public scandal. Baldwin acted swiftly and within a week Trenchard had sent for Lawrence and told him that he might now return to the Air Force. On 16th July 1925 the Chief of the Air Staff gave his formal approval to the transfer of Private T. E. Shaw to the R.A.F.

32

After eighteen months at Cranwell Cadet College, where he worked as an aircraft hand and in his spare time did the abridgment of his memoir that was published as *Revolt in the Desert,* Lawrence was transferred to India in December 1926 at his own request. He was not unhappy at Cranwell. On the contrary: his letters speak of having found a new home back in the Air Force. But he did not want to be around when *Revolt in the Desert* was published and to have to endure more publicity on that account.

However, in India trouble again dogged his footsteps. Indian officialdom was hardly to be expected to look with favour on the presence in its midst of the man who had done so much to destroy its ambitions in Mesopotamia during and after the war; so Lawrence was virtually "confined to barracks" during his stay at Karachi, his first Indian station, to keep him out of harm's way.

After more than a year of tedium at Karachi, only slightly relieved by the work of completing *The Mint,* he asked to be posted up country. His old friend from Arabian days, Air Marshal Salmond, was then Air Chief in India and, as a favour to Lawrence, agreed to his being sent to a R.A.F. outpost called Miranshah on the North-West Frontier. The station comprised a total Air Force complement of twenty-six men and five officers with a few hundred Indian scouts, and consisted of a brick and earth fort behind barbed wire situated in a ring of low blue hills "with chipped edges and a broken-bottle skyline." Ten miles from the Afghan border, it was a place of uncanny quietness and solitude, broken only by a nightly concert of jackals, a cool and blessed relief from the steamy climate of Karachi. But the move unhappily proved to be his undoing. He had not been there more than a month when, in spite of strenuous precautions, his presence in this embattled area of Britain's imperial domains became known to the American press, who had for long been looking for an exciting story to fasten onto his return to the East. The Soviet newspapers started an immediate outcry that Colonel Lawrence was spying in Afghanistan and the British Minister at Kabul requested that he be sent back to England. Relations between the Indian government and Aghanistan were then at a most sensitive point and Lawrence's continued presence on the Afghan border would have risked a serious incident.

He returned early in 1929 to a barrage of comment and speculation in Britain. Unfortunately for him, just before he was withdrawn from Miranshah, a rebellion broke out in Afghanistan which led to the deposition of the King. Labour politicians and the left-wing press in Britain became convinced that Lawrence, whom they had long suspected as being in reality a leading British intelligence agent masquerading as an ordinary airman, had engineered the Afghan conspiracy at the instigation of the government of India. Questions were asked in Parliament and, at a demonstration staged on Tower Hill by a group of Communists, Lawrence was burned in effigy!

Lawrence decided on his return to put a stop to this nonsensical publicity and went straight to the House of Commons where he saw the two ringleaders of the hue and cry, Mr. James Maxton and Mr. Ernest Thurtle, both members of the Independent Labour Party. He succeeded in convincing them that he was not a spy for any government and had had nothing whatever to do with the Afghan rising. The incident ended in laughter, when a day or so later the press announced that Colonel T. E. Lawrence had been received not "by", but "into" the Independent Labour Party—a joke that was not, it seems, appreciated by the Air Ministry.

Thereafter Lawrence found his niche in the Royal Air Force, in which he had signed on for a further five years from 1930. Trenchard, ever embarrassed by his presence, suggested a posting as far from London as possible. He proposed Scotland, but Lawrence thought this sounded too cold and wet and eventually agreed to be posted to the R.A.F. station at Cattewater on Plymouth Sound, later renamed "Mount Batten." Here he made two new friends; the first was his own Commanding Officer, Wing Commander Sydney Smith, whose understanding and humanity made him a minor "Allenby" to Lawrence: the second was Lady Astor, the Member of Parliament for Plymouth, whose house offered him a varied company of interesting men from every world from politics to the arts and provided him with intellectual stimulus whenever he needed it. He teased Lady Astor unmercifully, remarking for instance that Cattewater must have been named after her. But he also found her vitality at times exhausting and remarked to a friend that he would like her better if she were bedridden!

During this period Lawrence divided his time between helping to organize the Schneider Trophy seaplane races and developing fast motor-boats for air-sea rescue. The second of these tasks had started quite accidentally. One day he happened to be crossing Plymouth Sound in a R.A.F. motor launch when an aircraft from his station crashed in the water. Lawrence went to the rescue with his launch, but failed to get there in time to keep the aircraft afloat or save its trapped crew. The experience had a lasting effect on him and he determined to design a boat that would be fast enough to get to the scene of future crashes in time and would be equipped with a device to stop the aircraft sinking and so give time for the crew to escape.

Air-sea rescue was then a virtually unknown science; but, with the help and encouragement of Sydney Smith, Lawrence set about designing and testing motor-boats for this purpose. After some initial sales-resistance from the Air Ministry, Lawrence's idea caught on and, from then until the end of his R.A.F. service in 1935, he devoted most of his time to testing, designing and delivering these special fast craft. Many a pilot shot down in the sea in the Second World War probably owes his life to Lawrence's inspiration and work in this field.

Lawrence's part in organizing the Schneider Trophy races did not have as easy a run as his work with the motor-boats. In the summer of 1929 the Labour Party was returned again as the government of Britain and Lord Thomson became Secretary of State for Air once more. Irked by Lawrence's refusal to write the history of the R.A.F. without conditions, Thomson made little secret of the fact that he was only waiting for an opportunity to drop on Aircraftman Shaw and oust him from the service. The occasion arose when General Balbo, the Italian Air Minister and a guest of honour at the air races, was seen talking to Lawrence with all the intimacy of the old friend that he was. Following on this several other important political personalties of the Conservative Party were seen engaging Lawrence in conversation. On Thomson's instructions he was promptly served with notice of dismissal. Later, when influential friends had intervened, he was summoned before the unhappy Trenchard and told that he could only stay in the Air Force if in future he behaved like an ordinary aircraftman, confined himself to routine duties and gave up his contacts with such important personalities in the Opposition party as Churchill, Lord Birkenhead, Austen Chamberlain and Lady Astor!

Realizing that such a petty restriction could only be temporary, Lawrence agreed and devoted all his spare time to finishing the translation of Homer's *Odyssey* which had been commissioned from him by an American publisher, Mr. Bruce Rogers. By the time that he had completed the work at the end of 1930, the restrictions on his duties and leisure had lapsed and he was able to return with renewed zest to his speed-boats.

❖   ❖   ❖

A year before his engagement was due to end in 1935 Lawrence started to worry about his future. At this time he saw a great deal of his old friend from the days of Carchemish, Dr. Ernest Altounyan. In Altounyan's view, he was then completely "cured" of the mental breakdown which caused him to hide himself away in the Air Force, and acknowledged that he now owed it to his country to return to a normal life and taken up some work of national importance befitting his intellectual capacities. But his letters to his mother speak mournfully of his active life being over once he left the Air Force. "I am too young to be happy doing nothing, and too old to make a fresh start." Again to a friend, "I shall feel like a lost dog when I leave . . . the strange attraction in the feel of the clothes, the work, the companionship, a direct touch with men, obtained no other way in my life."

He underlined this feeling that his real life would end with his leaving the company of ordinary men in an "epitaph" upon himself which he wrote on his departure from the Air Force at the invitation of Robert Graves who had been asked by some newspaper to compile his obituary.

I have a deep sense that my life in the real sense is now over. . . . To me it is the multitude of road transport drivers filling all the roads of England every night who make this mechanical age. And it is the airmen, the mechanics, who are overcoming the air, not the Mollisons or Orlebars. The genius raids, but the common people occupy and possess. Wherefore I stayed in the ranks and served to the best of my ability, much influencing my fellow airmen towards a pride in themselves and their articulate duty. I tried to make them see—with some success.

Liddell Hart confirms his success when he says, "He was a greater spiritual force than the whole board of Chaplains in raising the standard of decency, fair play and unselfish comradeship." His last Commanding Officer, Wing Commander Sims, wrote that Lawrence was also instrumental in getting a number of reforms in the more petty and irritating disciplinary regulations of the R.A.F.

In March 1935 Lawrence said farewell to the Royal Air Force and retired to Clouds Hill. But the press were waiting for him when he returned home and he was forced to barricade himself inside for several days to escape their attentions, which even included throwing stones at the roof and windows of the cottage to get him to come out and submit to their questions and their cameras. After they had finally wearied off the pursuit, he settled down to "an empty life in this earthly paradise." "In this mood," he wrote to Lady Astor, "I would not take on any job at all. There is something broken in the works, as I told you: my will, I think."

Yet five days later, on 13th May, he received a letter from a friend, Henry Williamson, who fervently believed that England must seek an understanding with Germany. "You alone are capable of negotiating with Hitler," he wrote to Lawrence, "I must speak to you about this immediately." Lawrence rode his motor-cycle to the Bovington Post Office and sent off a telegram to Williamson: "Lunch Tuesday wet fine cottage one mile north Bovington camp."

Returning to Clouds Hill, he swerved to avoid two boys on bicycles and his machine skidded off the road. Lawrence never regained consciousness and six days later he died. He was buried in the cemetery at Moreton, a few miles from his cottage. Churchill, Storrs, Newcombe and Kennington were all present to see this great hero of England laid to rest in the Dorset soil that he loved so much. In recognition of his contribution to England's history and achievements, his bust stands in the Crypt of St. Paul's Cathedral in London, beside such men as Nelson, Wellington and Constable—heroes of war and of art, moulders of Britain's greatness, fitting company for the soldier and the artist that were combined in the person of T. E. Lawrence.

33

What was it that lay at the root of the Lawrence enigma? How are we to explain the actions and reactions of this strange creature who combined in a single character enough complexities and contradictions for a thousand other men?

Many a writer has tried to supply the answer to these questions and none has yet succeeded. Like everyone else who has had the temerity to set down his conclusions upon this baffling personality, I have consulted those of his friends and relatives who are still living and again found no real explanation of what made him do all the things that he did. Here and there, like a bloodhound on a cold scent, one may pick up something of a trail, only to find that it leads nowhere or that the vital connecting link to the next part of the explanation is missing and the trail has stopped.

Part of the reason for this is that, throughout his whole life, Lawrence never communicated the answer to a single other human being. Such fragmentary explanations as exist have emerged since his death from personal documents and from the testimony of friends. Also there has been in many analyses of his character a tendency to confuse the two main questions concerning his life. These were, in chronological order; first, what made him leave Damascus; and second, what drove him into the "monastery" of the Royal Air Force? It would obviously be nonsense to say that these two questions are in no way related, but there is also an important distinction between them. The first is largely a political issue with certain hard and definite facts to provide pointers; the second delves into altogether deeper problems—the interaction of the sensual, mental and spiritual processes within a tormented human being. Faced by these infinitely complex problems, a number of writers have been tempted to offer the simple "political" answer—Lawrence's sufferings over the betrayal of the Arabs—as the reason not only for his walking out on his triumph in Damascus but also for his determination to lose his shadow in the ranks of the R.A.F. This is not true, as an examination of the facts will show.

Certainly it was his desperate disappointment and sense of failure in Damascus which made him turn his back on the victory which he had done so much to achieve. He was sick of playing the fraud, sick of the feuds, jealousies and treacheries of the Arabs, sick of Allied perfidy, hurt by Feisal's ingratitude, and mentally and physically near to breaking point. His Arab war had begun as a prank to escape from the tedium of the map-room at G.H.Q. Then, with the discovery of Feisal, it had become a dream, inspired with a sense of mission to help the Arabs to liberate Arabia. Ambition beckoned, promising glittering prizes, power and prestige and Lawrence saw himself as the kingmaker and Feisal's right hand in a free Syria. Then came a jolt—the discovery of the Allies' plans to parcel out Arabia between them in contradiction of their promises of independence to the Arabs. But success followed rapidly—advance in the Hejaz and then the high point of daring achievement, Akaba—and with success came confidence in Arab strength and unity. *"El Aurens"* was acclaimed as a legend among the tribes, whose eager cheers rang louder than the nagging little voice of conscience that kept whispering "fraud" in his ear. The Arabs would wrest their freedom from all who challenged them. They would see to this in Damascus.

Then one day the dream turned into a nightmare.

Lawrence realized that the unity among the tribes that Feisal had contrived was but a façade behind which the Sherifian family were hatching their conspiracies to do him down. Gone was his last hope that the Arabs would be able to defend the freedom they were about to win from the Turks. Gone were his ambitions, his sense of mission. Knowing how the Allies planned to apportion the Arab world between themselves after Turkey's defeat, any victory could now only be for him a hollow sham; and when it came, it only required the additional humiliation of Feisal's evident desire to be rid of his servant to determine Lawrence to leave Damascus without a moment's delay.

But almost immediately after his escape he was dragged back into the cockpit of Arab and Allied politics, first by Feisal and later by Churchill. And, although to begin with it seemed that his return to the arena was to meet with an even more bitter failure at the Peace Conference, we later have it from Lawrence's own pen that, at Cairo in 1921, all the wrongs done to the Arabs which could be redressed were put right and England was "out of the Arab affair with clean hands." Yet a year after he had, according to this his own statement, secured the fulfilment of Britain's pledges to the Arabs and so redeemed his honour, he enlisted in the R.A.F. under an assumed name. It can scarcely be said therefore that his reasons for entering the "monastery" of the Air Force were the same as those which prompted his departure from Damascus—a sense of disgust and dishonour over the Allies' betrayal of Feisal.

What then is the answer to the "second" question? What compulsion drove him to escape a second time? The publicity that followed the Lowell Thomas lectures? Hardly likely, for the embarrassment that this sudden notoriety caused him was largely superficial; and Lawrence's problem was far deeper than a mere surface embarrassment. Was it insanity? Again the answer is no. Lawrence talked a lot about his sanity at the time of his enlistment; and it is also said that the five brothers once made a vow never to marry because of a fear that there was insanity in the family. But even if this were a credible explanation—and certainly the cool and deliberate manner in which Lawrence set about organizing his life after the war belies the suggestion that he was mad—there still remains the question, what made him insane and drove him to such extraordinary limits of self-degradation?

More than one writer has sought to explain the enigma by asserting that Lawrence was a tortured homosexual. But no one has ever produced any evidence to prove this assertion. In fact everybody who knew him well has stated categorically and without hesitation that Lawrence was not homosexual. Robert Graves, Dr. Altounyan, Kirkbride, Colonel Joyce, Mrs. Kennington, David Garnett, Basil Liddell Hart and the late Colonel Newcombe—to name only a few of his closest friends—all agree on this. Besides, and perhaps most conclusively of all the evidence, there was never the smallest suggestion of homosexuality throughout the time that Lawrence spent in the R.A.F. and the Tank Corps, living among an entirely male company over the space of more than twelve years. David Garnett has also publicly stated that he once saw a letter from Lawrence addressed to a homosexual which showed clearly that, while he had no moral objection, he regarded the idea of a homosexual relationship as physically repellent.

In fact, according to the best testimony available, the shock of being told of his illegitimacy created in him a revulsion towards sex. If physical desire could bring upon him and his brothers the shame of bastardy, he wanted to have nothing to do with any form of sex. His aversion was further stimulated by an experience which he suffered at school and which produced in him a horror of physical contact with any other human being.

This evidence equally disposes of the story that

Lawrence was in love with a Jewish lady, called Sarah Aaronsohn—a British secret agent living behind the Turkish lines at the time of the Arab revolt. According to this piece of fantasy, having been flogged into impotence at Deraa, Lawrence renounced his love and this was the cause of his tragedy. From this it is concluded that the love poem entitled "To S.A." which serves as a dedication of the *Seven Pillars of Wisdom* was written by Lawrence for Sarah Aaronsohn. But this romantic legend does not unfortunately stand up. Apart from Lawrence's vow of abstinence, official enquiries have revealed that the two never met and never could have met. Sarah Aaronsohn was in Palestine while Lawrence was alternately in Egypt, the Hejaz and southern Transjordan and she died in a Turkish prison in March 1917, eight months before Lawrence's own capture and torture at Deraa.

Lawrence never explained who or what "S.A." represented—or rather he gave several contradictory explanations to different people. To some he said that the initials represented "a person now dead"; to others, he said that one letter corresponded to a person, the other to a place; and, to Robert Graves, he suggested that "S.A." was Sheikh Ahmed, the young Arab boy whom he knew in Syria before the war. To confuse the issue still further, it has been suggested that Sheikh Ali also rates consideration for the solution of the puzzle after Lawrence's description of their relationship as that of "David and Jonathan." But in fact it is far more likely that "S.A." was an imaginary conception, unrelated to a particular person or place, which represented all that he had found that was fair and gentle and lovable in Arabia and its peoples. One thing at least is certain; this minor riddle offers neither clue nor connection to the main enigma of Lawrence's life.

It is my own firm conviction that the key to the enigma is to be found in a combination of three things—masochism, fear of responsibility and mental breakdown. Lawrence was a physical and mental masochist. Overwhelming evidence to this effect is to be found in his own writings, in private diaries and in his actions during and after the First World War. To quote one such admission in the *Seven Pillars of Wisdo*m, "I punished my flesh cheerfully, finding greater sensuality in the punishment than in the sin, so much was I intoxicated with pride at not sinning simply." In another commentary on his Arabian experiences he wrote that "pain was a solvent, a cathartic, almost a decoration to be fairly worn." Also several of his friends have confirmed that there was a strong streak of masochism in his make-up. Kirkbride for one has said that Lawrence "liked to drive himself without mercy; in fact, I suspect that he loved suffering." David Garnett also shares this view. Indeed it would scarcely be possible and certainly most unlikely that anyone would have driven himself as hard as Lawrence, had he not got some masochistic delight from the punishment.

For a man of less extraordinary background and character than Lawrence the discovery that he was a masochist would probably not involve a spiritual collapse. But it has to be remembered that ever since he learned of his illegitimate birth Lawrence had led anything but an ordinary life, having renounced sex because of the shame that it had brought upon him and his family. The combination of his own continence with the background of his puritanical upbringing could of itself be sufficient reason for the discovery that he found a perverted sensual pleasure in pain to come as a considerable shock. But there was another far more complicated and more compelling reason for the anguish which he had suffered and from which he never fully recovered.

There is reason to believe that early in the desert campaign Lawrence began to think of himself as some kind of new Messiah sent to save the world from tyranny and oppression. Always introspective, he had worried over and over again at the question, why am I here and who sent me? He had sent himself; but that was no answer. Then somewhere along the line of this reasoning, Lawrence, for whom modesty was not exactly a strong suit, began to compare his own life and antecedents with those of the Messiah Himself. There was the question mark about his birth; he was waging a war for a great cause by preaching rather than by fighting: he had undergone the temptations in the wilderness, had been offered the Kingdom from the high mountain and had renounced the flesh and the devil: he was fêted and worshipped everywhere as a saviour by an excited and adoring populace, reaching out to touch the hem of his garment and crying his name, *"El Aurens, El Aurens"*: he had performed near miracles in the capture of Akaba, the ride across Sinai and the welding together of feuding tribes: and when, as at Aba el Lissan and in other actions, he had been forced to draw his sword, he had afterwards felt only pity for the slain enemy and distaste for the greed of the victors.

This much of course is mere supposition based on reading between the lines of his own memoir. But a strange confirmation of the theory is to be found in Lawrence's reaction to one of the Kennington sketches for the privately printed edition of the *Seven Pillars of Wisdom*. The drawing, entitled "Strata," is of Lawrence as a god-head above the clouds looking down upon a scene of struggle on earth representing the Arab revolt. Lawrence was utterly amazed when Kennington showed him this drawing and kept repeating that he could not believe that anyone could have captured so completely what at times he had felt about himself during the desert campaign. Another known fact is that at the outset of his Arabian adventure he was also in the habit of scourging himself. His explanation of this was that he believed that he would one day be called upon to suffer some terrible torture and was training himself to be able to withstand whatever pain might be inflicted upon him.

It was in this exalted frame of mind that he entered Deraa on that fateful day in November 1917. When the Turks began to beat him he felt that his premonition had been correct and he would endure his torture like a true Messiah, inured to pain by the power of his spirit and his will. Then came the shattering awakening, as, in his own words, he realized that "a delicious warmth, probably sexual, was swelling through me" and he knew that he was no risen prophet, no Son of God, but a rabid masochist, whose happy endurance of pain disclosed a perversion of the flesh rather than a triumph of the spirit. Thus exposed to himself and mocked by his tormentors, he broke down and submitted to their pleasure.

In the Oxford edition of the *Seven Pillars of Wisdom,* Lawrence described the immediate aftermath of this horrifying revelation in these words;

It could not have been my defilement for no one ever held the body in less honour than I did myself. Probably it had been the breaking of the spirit by the frenzied nerve-shattering pain which had degraded me to beast level when it made me grovel to it and which had journeyed with me since, a fascination and morbid desire, lascivious and vicious perhaps but like the striving of a moth towards its flame.

This soul-searing confession of his masochism was deleted from the subscribers' edition, where he merely spoke of having lost "the citadel of my integrity" in Deraa. But there was no way of striking out of his mind the effect of so shattering and degrading a revelation of himself. From then on he became a changed man, hard and bitter in his judgment of himself and others and ruthless in his actions. As he revealed in his self-analysis in the desert and in the epilogue to his memoir, he had suddenly run out of spiritual fuel, his sense of mission was lost and his motors were henceforward driven by an unvarnished ambition and lust for power. To this end he used quite ruthlessly his extraordinary, even uncanny, powers of leadership, often driving himself and his Arabs beyond the limits of endurance, hating himself for the fraud that he now knew himself to be, yet striving relentlessly towards the temporal rewards that loomed disproportionately large in the wake of his spiritual divestment.

Then came the day when he discovered that even these ambitions were built on a delusion. His dream of power was ended and his purpose had turned into a tragic farce. In a last horrifying convulsion he became a killer, living in a nightmare world of blood-lust, until a slap in the face from an imbecile brought the nightmare to an end. As the bloodshot mists cleared from his brain, he knew that he was finished, spent and utterly exhausted in mind and body. He could only think of ridding himself of responsibility, of escaping from the trap of his own leadership. As Dr. Altounyan has written, describing his first reunion with Lawrence after the war, "I found a man . . . shaken by his vision, not of past accomplishment, but of incredible possibilities which unless he was very careful could become, were becoming, actualities leading to regions where he instinctively felt it would be terribly dangerous to remain." That a part of him wanted to remain, once the worst effects of his exhaustion had worn off, is clear from his own appreciation of himself and from his subsequent brief return to the arena in Paris, Cairo and Transjordan. But the very lust for power that lingered in his heart made it the more imperative to his rational self to escape from these "dangerous regions" and in his own words "to make me impossible for anyone to suggest for a responsible position."

Lawrence's problem was undoubtedly made more acute because he was never able to talk to anyone about it. Had he lived in this day and age of psychiatry it is still by no means certain that he would have sought medical aid. But since such help was not in any case available to him, he sought his own cure— enlistment in the Royal Air Force, where he hoped to rediscover that bond of common humanity which in the desert he had found so infinitely preferable to the company of his social equals. Here he would find a new security in subservience and forget the nightmare of self-deception to which his years of responsibility had brought him.

But his life in the ranks, at least in the beginning, was a sad disappointment. Instead of the simple understanding soldiers he had known in the war, he found himself among men whom he did not understand and officers whom he could not respect. Yet he could not go back now, for he had forsworn his Arabian past. Even when he was thrown out, he knew he must get into the R.A.F. again and see his cure through. His honour was too deeply involved and, besides, the masochist in him rejoiced at the misery of his soul and the sufferings of his battered body. The violence done to his spirit by bawling, brutal N.C.O.s and a licentious company of men, not to speak of the agonies of physical training, gave him a strange pleasure. "There is nothing so restful," he wrote to his mother, "as taking orders from fools." In letters to Lionel Curtis he spoke of "my masochism" as his reason for staying in the forces and of "self-degradation" as his reason for enlisting in the ranks.

What then is one to conclude from the end of the story? Was the cure a success or did he emerge from the Air Force still a broken man? That he was cured sufficiently to enable him to take up life again and assume a position of responsibility is very doubtful. He wanted it to be thought that he was going to return. Hence his anxiety that it should be known that he had been offered the Secretaryship of the Committee of Imperial Defence and other high-ranking positions. But his fears at leaving the "monastery" and facing the world and his conviction that his life was really over do not suggest a man bursting to take part in affairs of state.

Yet there was one element of his old self that the long years of recuperation were able fully to restore or rather to direct into a new "safe" channel. The power of leadership, which he feared so much in himself, found a fresh and constructive outlet in its influence upon the lives of his friends, old and new. Not only did he understand their problems with a sympathy made the greater by his own suffering, but he was able also to show them the solution best suited to their own character and complexities. Many are the tributes which have been paid to his gentle understanding and capacity to uplift and help other people to find the way which he had lost. Perhaps no one put it quite so well as Gertrude Bell: "He lit so many fires in cold rooms."

ALDINGTON, Richard, *Lawrence of Arabia,* London, Collins, 1955.

BIRDWOOD, Lord, *Nuri es Said,* London, Cassels, 1959.

GARNETT, David (Ed.), *The Essential T. E. Lawrence,* London, Jonathan Cape, 1951.

—(Ed.), *The Letters of T. E. Lawrence,* London, Jonathan Cape, 1938.

GRAVES, Robert, *Lawrence and the Arabs,* London, Jonathan Cape, 1927.

GRAVES, Robert, and LIDDELL HART, B. H., *T. E. Lawrence to his Biographers,* London, Faber & Faber, 1938.

KIRKBRIDGE, Sir Alec, *A Crackle of Thorns,* London, John Murray, 1956.

LAWRENCE, A. W. (Ed.), *T. E. Lawrence by his Friends,* London, Jonathan Cape, 1937.

—(Ed.), *Oriental Assembly,* London, Williams & Norgate, 1939.

LAWRENCE, M. R. (Ed.), *The Home Letters of T. E. Lawrence and his Brothers,* Oxford, Blackwell, 1954.

LAWRENCE, T. E., *Seven Pillars of Wisdom,* Oxford Edition, 1922.

—*Seven Pillars of Wisdom,* London, Jonathan Cape, 1935.

—*Revolt in the Desert,* London, Jonathan Cape, 1927.

—*The Mint,* London, Jonathan Cape, 1955.

LIDDELL HART, B. H., *T. E. Lawrence—in Arabia and After,* London, Jonathan Cape, 1934.
See also under Graves *above.*

PHILBY, H. St. John, *Forty Years in the Wilderness,* London, Robert Hale, 1957.

STIRLING, Col. W. F., *Safety Last,* London, Hollis & Carter, 1953.

STORRS, Sir Ronald, *Orientations,* London, Nicholson & Watson, 1939.

THOMAS, Lowell, *With Lawrence in Arabia,* New York and London, Century Co., 1924.

VILLARS, Jean Beraud, *T. E. Lawrence,* London, Sedgwick & Jackson, 1958.

B

C

SIGNET True Adventure and History

THE HERO OF IWO JIMA and Other Stories
by William Bradford Huie

The story of the tragic American Indian and war hero, Ira Hayes, coming as a film called "The Outsider," starring Tony Curtis; also an account of the Chessman Case and other important news stories. (#D2091—50¢)

SILENT SERVICE   *by William C. Chambliss*

True stories of submarine warfare in the Pacific, based on scripts of the popular television program of the same name. (#S1658—35¢)

THE STRANGE ORDEAL OF THE S. S. NORMANDIER
by H. L. Tredree

An eye-witness account of the terrifying voyage of a fever-stricken ship and the dying crew who struggled to keep her afloat. (#S1751—35¢)

SUBMARINE!   *by Edward L. Beach*

A heart-stirring account of submarine warfare in the Pacific during World War II. (#D1837—50¢)

THOSE DEVILS IN BAGGY PANTS   *by Ross S. Carter*

The gallant, thrilling experiences of twelve paratroopers in Africa and Europe. (#D2056—50¢)

BATTLE: THE STORY OF THE BULGE   *by John Toland*

A dramatic reconstruction—hour by hour, move by move—of the most controversial battle of World War II. Illustrated. (#T1862—75¢)

THE MEMOIRS OF FIELD MARSHAL MONTGOMERY

The autobiography of one of the most colorful and spectacular generals of World War II. (#T1741—75¢)

THE EXECUTION OF PRIVATE SLOVIK
by William Bradford Huie

The story of the only American soldier to be shot for desertion in World War II. (#1113—25¢)

Outstanding SIGNET War Novels

THE YOUNG LIONS   by Irwin Shaw
   The famous bestseller about war's impact on three soldiers—two Americans and a German.   (#T1496—75¢)

THE ANGRY HILLS   by Leon Uris
   A hard-hitting novel of adventure, set against the background of war-torn Greece and the desperate struggle
   between the Nazi invaders and the patriot underground.
   By the author of the bestselling *Exodus* and *Mila 18*.
                                         (#D1879—50¢)

FROM HERE TO ETERNITY   by James Jones
   The magnificent bestseller about army life in Hawaii
   before Pearl Harbor.   (#Q1967—95¢)

THE NAKED AND THE DEAD   by Norman Mailer
   The famous novel about fighting men sent on an impossible Pacific mission.   (#T1549—75¢)

BAND OF BROTHERS   by Ernest Frankel
   The thrilling account of one company of Marines caught
   in the deadly, mid-winter retreat from the Yalu during
   the Korean War, and the commanding officer who had
   to prove himself to his men.   (#D1780—50¢)

BREAD AND WINE   by Ignazio Silone
   This suspenseful, compassionate and humorous story of
   the Italian underground, a plea for a new society and a
   new humanity, has been hailed as one of the great novels
   of the twentieth century.   (#D1545—50¢)

THE PISTOL   by James Jones
   An exciting novel about a G.I. who acquires a pistol the
   day the Japanese bomb Pearl Harbor, and the men who
   try to get it away from him.   (#D1893—50¢)

Other SIGNET Novels You'll Enjoy

THE GENERAL   by Alan Sillitoe

A powerful parable of mankind's drive to self-destruction —the story of a General ordered to shoot an entire symphony orchestra, captured accidentally in total war. By the author of *Saturday Night and Sunday Morning*.

(#D2077—50¢)

JOURNEY NOT TO END   by Paul Herr

The grim and suspenseful search of a concentration-camp survivor for his ravaged identity.   (#P2075—60¢)

THE MANCHURIAN CANDIDATE   by Richard Condon

A Korean War hero, diabolically brainwashed in a Chinese prison, returns home to become the center of political intrigue and an assassin against his will.

(#D1630—50¢)

NO TIME FOR SERGEANTS   by Mac Hyman

The hilarious misadventures of a Georgia cracker in the army.   (#D1530—50¢)

GO NAKED IN THE WORLD   by Tom T. Chamales

The robust novel of an embittered young war hero who revolts against his family and society. A smash-hit movie starring Gina Lollobrigida and Anthony Franciosa.

(#T1878—75¢)

SOLDIER'S PAY   by William Faulkner

Passion and death mingle in the Nobel Prize winner's novel about a returned veteran.   (#P2006—60¢)

THE DECEIVERS   by Richard Goldhurst

A wounded veteran, transformed by plastic surgery, becomes an impostor, and discovers a hidden crime.

(#S1958—35¢)

How To Build
A Low-Cost Library

You can build a personal library of the best books for as little as 35 or 50 cents a volume. Choose from thousands of the classics and best sellers in literature, biography, poetry, art, history, religion, reference, and science as listed in a new catalog:

Paperbound Books in Print

If you've often had trouble finding the paperbacks you want—here are over 14,500—with information on how and where to get them. Here you can locate all the low-priced paper books available either by checking the thousands of titles listed alphabetically by author and by title, or by looking under any of the 90 categories where selected titles are grouped under helpful subject classification.

Order your copy of this unique buying guide today—either from your dealer or direct from RRB, New American Library of World Literature, 501 Madison Avenue, New York 22, N. Y.

If you order from New American Library please make checks payable to: R. R. Bowker Company. Single copies are $3 net prepaid, or you can subscribe to the 4 quarterly issues for just $8 a year and automatically be kept up to date on available paperbacks.